Papa Was a Promise Keeper

by Rose Grindheim Sims

PAPA WAS A PROMISE KEEPER

ISBN: 1-882415-02-7

New Life Church Growth Ministries, Inc.
34631 Orchid Parkway, Ridge Manor, Florida 33525

To Papa,

immigrant, pioneer, trailblazer,
humble Christian saint,
promise keeper,
who taught us all
to serve God more faithfully,
to give and not count the cost,
to conquer and not heed the wounds,
to toil and not seek for rest,
to labor and not ask for any reward save
that of knowing that we do God's will.
He put his hand to the plow and never
looked back. May his tribe increase.

This book is also dedicated to Rosanna,
Ben, Victoria Rose and Ron, Papa's great-
grandchildren, who are the poorer for
never having known Papa.
May his faith increase their faith.

Jesus replied, "No one who puts his hand to the
plow and looks back is fit for service in the
kingdom of God" (Luke 9:62).

Contents

Preface

Remembering Papa

*L*ong before 50,000 cheering, foot-stomping men showed up at Anaheim Stadium not to watch the California Angels play but to strengthen the family and restore the nation by becoming "promise keepers instead of promise breakers," there were heroes like Papa . . . the promise keeper.

America was built on immigrant Papas like mine who knew that "a man's man is a godly man." Papa's search for identity ended when he found Christ.

Until the 1950s, the family structure in America remained intact. Since then, radical feminism has done much to destroy the family. Concerned women have been careful to distinguish between "feminism" and "radical feminism." Feminism correctly protests violence against women, unequal pay, and discrimination in the job market. Feminism is dead wrong, however, when it robs men of their rightful place in our homes and society. Tremendous changes have occurred since my Papa set foot on American soil. Heroes are getting harder to find.

Some thinkers are predicting that the greatest and longest movement of the twenty-first century may be the men's movement. This movement will not stop at integrating African American and Hispanic men into a system that already exists. The movement will generate an evolutionary shift in the system itself to restore to men, women, and children their God-given places in the family.

In the struggle for equality, have we women unconsciously undermined genuine equality? The average man has always had both great value and power—more than he could dream. It staggers the imagination. The feminist movement has chosen to dwell on the dark side of men and for that we are the poorer. The potential for good in men is equally deep, and there is a great unfilled void in the lives of both men and women who ignore this possibility.

Too often, men are ridiculed for being men. The media portrays them as sitcom buffoons, heartless, money-loving, lustful and angry. The strident criticism from the feminist movement has left men feeling powerless and frustrated, unsure of their role in the family and beyond.

Women have written too few books about the incredible value of men. The truth is that what men really want is not corporate power, royal treatment, or wild experiences. They are looking for honest communication, balance in life's demands, deeply meaningful relationships, and the capacity to be respected as true fathers and mentors—as promise keepers. Unless they realize this, women miss vital relationships, confidants, quality husbands and fathers, and balance in their lives. It is time to minimize gender war and maximize gender love.

When we get lost it is important to retrace our steps. As you share Papa's story perhaps you will recover from your past a similar hero whose steps you and your posterity can recall. He may have been a pioneer, a trailblazer, a promise keeper who can recapture tomorrow for us all.

When life is over and our work on earth is done, there will be two kinds of people: those who say "Thank God I did" and those who say "If only I had." This book is written to help us all to better say "Thank God I did."

Chapter One

For Whom the Bells Toll

*H*olger Voetmann laid a heavy hand on the rusty third-hand, three-horse gang plow which he had recently and expertly repaired for the umpteenth time with nothing but barbed wire. The old horses, wearily leaned into the harness to accommodate yet another hour of grueling torture. Since early sunup the scorching ball of fire overhead had beaten down relentlessly on the stubborn virgin prairie and the young immigrant farmer who was seeking to conquer it with sheer wit and determination. Before him scurried earth-colored prairie dogs shaking their fists angrily at the one who dared to disturb their territorial domain.

Wearing a sunbonnet, swinging a syrup pail containing *rullepølse* sandwiches Mama had made on coarse Danish rye bread from the last of this year's meager harvest, I could see Papa in the distance. I was bringing supper to my Papa who would not come home until he had turned the last possible furrow in the rapidly diminishing twilight. Back and forth, back and forth the old syrup pail swung! Back and forth Papa plowed to the rhythm of the vesper bells pealing from the Danish Lutheran Church in the village.

I was four that year, red-haired, freckle-faced, wondering if it were really true that we would move to Wisconsin, away from the stumps and stones, Russian thistles, wild blueberries and rutabaga fields. Most of all I wondered how we could leave the magnificent church with the tall white tapers and the golden vesper bells. How could we leave the friendly folks who spoke Danish, even to go to a land where Mama said there were no rocks and where she promised for sure there would be absolutely no more trouble? Was there really such a hiding place in life? And was there honestly a farm with no stumps and stones, a promised land with a two-story house and a hip-roofed barn just like in Denmark? And was there ever a place without trouble?

Tonight while Papa was eating I would have him alone for just a few minutes and could ask him. As Papa came to the end of the row he waved to me and called out, "Ah, my little Rose. Did you hear the bells?"

I ran to meet him. He reached down and patted my red hair, then swooped me up in his arms for a wonderful hug.

"Why do the bells ring, Papa?"

He did not answer until he was seated comfortably on the thick buffalo grass and had pulled off his heavy, sweaty work boots. "The bells are heavenly. But it's too much like the preaching. The *prest* (preacher) tells us many things about God. He uses sublime words, like the sound of those bells. But who will tell us not just about God but how to find him?"

"Does God hear the bells?" I asked.

"They say he hears a twig snap," Papa replied.

While I unpacked his lunch Papa stretched out on the grass and looked up at the azure blue sky which was laced with cumulus clouds. "God is hiding," Papa continued. "Many long years I have searched for him, inside the church and outside the church, in the old country and in the new country."

"What if you never find him?" I asked. "Then where will we go when we die?"

"*Ack, ja,* we don't need God just for dying—I could use a little heavenly help to get through living!"

Papa sat up. With the same resolute, determined look I had seen on his face in difficult situations he told me, "I'll make you a promise, little one. I promise I will find him! And when I do, when I know for certain that I am a child of God, I promise you—on my honor—that nobody I love or know will ever have to search as hard for God as I have."

The church bells' angelus concluded.

"Gone silent," Papa observed, almost to himself. "God has gone silent just like those bells."

But the bells had not gone silent. I was happy as I heard them begin to ring again. Maybe God was answering Papa's prayer after all.

But this time the bells were not chiming in a melodic rhythm. They were making an eerie, mournful tolling sound.

Clang! Pause.

Clang! Pause.

Slowly, ponderously, each stroke was allowed to all but die away into the distance before the next began. It was strange to a child's ears.

"*En, to, tre, fera,*" Papa counted.

"Why do the bells ring again?" I wondered.

"Someone has died," Papa answered softly, continuing to count, endlessly it seemed to me, until the bells once more fell silent.

"Whoever died was ninety-one," Papa said.

He looked away for a long moment, gazing once more in the direction of the church steeple. Then he looked back at me. With a touch of gladness he told me, "You will have eighty-seven years to be that age."

"Eighty-seven years until I have to think about death," I thought to myself.

I was frightened of death. It seemed Papa was also afraid of death, otherwise why the determined promise to find God?

"Thank God we didn't lose you . . ." Papa mused.

As he resumed eating, I began thinking about what he had said. What was dying like? Already in my young life I had almost died twice. What would have happened if I had died before finding

God? Where was heaven? Was it really filled with harps and golden streets and angel choirs? Who went there, and who did not go?

I wasn't sure I would not rather have my spirit go to the beautiful birch tree forest filled with singing nightingales in the old country Papa talked of so often. That would be heaven enough for me, to enter the Danish woodland with the sound of Papa singing, welcoming me home!

I wanted to ask him about the bells—the traditional death knell Danish immigrants had brought with them to the new world—but I knew from the promise he had just made to me that it was something he did not understand either. I changed the subject.

"Will we be moving to the Wisconsin place like Mama says?"

Papa sighed and was silent for a moment. He stared at the stone fence rows he had laboriously dug to clear the few hard won acres of newly plowed virgin buffalo grass. I thought at first he did not choose to answer me.

"Mama says we will leave Minnesota," he said at last. "If Mama says," he gestured with both hands, "what else is it?"

"Will there be a big house and a great barn, and will we be rich like she remembers from Denmark? And will there really be no stumps and stones to dig? Will Wisconsin be beautiful, like Denmark . . . Maybe even a little bit like heaven?"

Papa shrugged his shoulders. "Mama is wise. Wiser than I am. It's a bit of the king's blood she has in her veins, you know. She lived with her family on a *herre gård* manor estate back in the old country.

"When we first came here we lived in a chicken coop, with a floor of sand that the furniture sank into, until I could build the snug little house we have now." He took a deep breath. "When you have feasted on venison, you have little appetite for porridge."

Papa stood tall to stretch each work-weary limb. Then he reached down to pat my red hair and stroke my freckled cheeks again.

"Papa, I love you so much. I wish we could be like this always, you and me and the meadowlarks singing."

I knew Mama said we had to move because she thought nobody liked her in this place. Papa never talked about it. I wanted to ask him about this, but I didn't want to disturb the magic moment.

Why can't everyone get along? I thought.

It was time to go to work again. Papa stretched forward, his great bulging muscles leaning into the plow as if to lighten the strain for *Gammel Hesten,* the ancient bony and bedraggled dray horses that would have long ago been sold for dog food on a proper *herre gård* in the old country. As he toiled, Papa sang, *"Trygare kan ingen vara . . ."*

I joined him, my voice soft so I could keep in time with his:

Children of the heavenly father
Safely in His bosom gather.
Nestling bird nor star in Heaven
Such a refuge e'er was given.

Although I knew Mama would scold me, I remained in the field a little longer and greeted Papa each time he came to the end of a furrow. When his plow hit rocks that hindered progress, I thought of Wisconsin as a land of perfect soil. Maybe it was best that our family move. As Papa moved away from me, he seemed lost in a cloud of dust. I thought of Papa's promise. Someday Papa would find God and I would be one of those included in the promise. Papa always kept his promises!

But what if the bells rang for us before either of us found God? I shuddered. No, that could not happen. Papa was a promise keeper.

But now Mama was calling me to come home to do my chores.

Chapter Two

To the Golden Shore

*I*f Holger drank the bitter dregs of disappointment as he plowed row after endless row, if he dreamed of a flaxen-haired lassie who lived across the wide Atlantic—the girl he had courted for ten years then in bitter disappointment was forced to leave behind—he told no one.

"Ten long backbreaking years I worked for her father to earn enough money for land," he muttered, almost surprised at his own voice. For so many years he had blotted out the memory.

But today had been arduous. The pig-headed plow had broken again and again. A quick morning shower had left him damp. The sun had not shone except during the brief supper he had shared with his special little girl. Perhaps as an escape, he let his thoughts drift back in time.

Tonight in his imagination it seemed that Denmark was just yesterday and he was young and full of hope and dreams. He could almost see Rosa's overbearing, pompous father, Hans, storming into supper out of breath that fateful night so long ago. Panting, he informed Holger and the other hired hands that *Gaasejer* Ole Sorenson, owner of the neighboring *herre gård,* had been killed by lightning during that afternoon's thunderstorm.

The announcement brought a strange, foreboding hush. For hundreds of years the two manors had sat side by side. Their rich black loam, great herds of milk cows, and fertile fields were like two empires. As eldest sons, their owners—Hans Hansen and Ole Sorenson—competed fiercely for status and stature even though both had had the enviable good fortune of inheriting position and land.

All that was now over. Hans Hansen announced the news of his rival's demise with a twinge of glee as if he were reporting a rise in the daily price of cattle.

Holger marveled at the man's callousness. Those two men had been neighbors from childhood. They had played together. They worshipped each Sabbath in the same church, listened to the same sermons of love from the parish priest.

Both men had seemed to Holger to be cut from the same cloth. Holger was sure that the only way Hans had ever excelled Ole was, ironically, in siring a daughter, Rosa, who was as gentle and beautiful as her father was unyielding and portentous.

No one could hold a candle to Rosa, not in beauty or spirit. Rosa was a beam of summer sunlight on the cloudiest day. Ole Sorenson's only son, Nels, on the other hand, was the exact opposite. He was a menacing, bombastic, inflated parasite living off the fat of his father's assets and inherited status.

But Hans Hansen was not finished delivering his unexpected news to the hired men. "Nels has inherited it all!" he reported excitedly. "One strike of lightning from the hand of the Almighty and Nels owns it all, lock, stock, and barrel."

Why is he telling me this? Holger wondered. *Surely Hans is not comparing me with Nels. Well, thank God Rosa and I have been engaged for ten years and that is settled.*

"Well, Holger, what do you think?"

Holger thought, *I'm thinking that God is not fair. If I had that manor, Rosa and I would not have to wait any longer.* But he did not voice those thoughts. Instead he said, "What do I think? I think Nels is the poorest excuse for a man in all of Denmark. In no time he will have that farm in shambles. He sleeps until noon. He drinks until daybreak and squanders money like a drunken sailor."

"Nonsense," Hans roared. "Nels may not be perfect, but he can hire men to run the *gård.* Think of that, Holger. Nels has just become the most eligible bachelor in all of Denmark!"

Icy fear gripped Holger's heart, a frantic panic that he had never known before. He knew Hans was competitive but he also knew Rosa was his only daughter and the apple of his eye. Surely he could not stand to see her wed a buffoon like Nels.

If only I knew God, Holger thought. *If only I knew he answered prayers. If only I could ask him for a miracle.*

Just when he needed God most, God seemed far away, cold and impersonal . . . a long grey oblong he could not reach. He had searched with all his heart during the endless sermons in the village church when he sat with the hired hands and Rosa had to sit between her parents.

Hans Hansen was mighty benevolent to the new widow at Ole's funeral. On Monday he had been seen on business at the Sorenson's *gård*.

All week Holger called on a God who seemed to be a stone wall. Rosa was sent to her grandmother's home on the coast. Holger saw her only briefly at the end of the week when she slipped him a note at supper. It read:

> My darling Holger. I cannot live without you. We must marry at once. Papa is going to Sorenson's again tonight. Meet me in the stable as soon as he leaves.

That night, enfolded in his arms, she sobbed like a tiny, frail reed in a winter snowstorm. Yes, they decided they must marry at once. As soon as her father returned from Sorensons, they would confront him and insist that he let them marry now.

"We must act at once before Father destroys us both," she sobbed. "Papa has talked to *Fru* Sorenson about giving me to Nels."

The words exploded like a ton of dynamite in his heart.

"No—not Nels, that bumbling idiot! Your Papa would never do that to you. He loves you and we have been promised for ten years. It is just that no matter how hard I work, I never have enough money to buy enough land to satisfy your Papa. When is enough enough? Tonight we must take matters into our own hands."

"Papa said it will never be enough until you have as much land as Sorensons. He said if I marry Nels we will forever unite our two dynasties and I will be as rich as any Lord or Lady. Oh, Holger, without you I would forever be the poorest peasant in Denmark. The land is Satan's curse straight from hell."

"Dear, dear Rosa, I love you so. It will do no good to talk to your father. We will take the money I have saved and escape to America. There your Papa cannot control us. In America we can get more land than both your family and Sorensons own absolutely free just by proving up the land and living on it five years."

A brilliant moon shone through the birch trees and a nightingale sang softly in the willows. He pressed his lips to hers and held her tightly as if in that embrace nothing could ever come between them.

"Yes, Holger, the ship's captain can marry us. But we must hurry. I will pack my little steamer trunk tonight. You see about the tickets tomorrow. A boat is leaving in three days. We must not arouse suspicion. To live with Nels would be a prison sentence for life. Oh, Jesus, help me," Rosa pleaded to the Almighty.

"Rooosssaa! Rooosssaa! *Kom nu!*" Hans bellowed from the kitchen house. Holger could hear Rosa's father's lumbering steps. Their eternity hung on this moment.

"Rosa, my love. Are you sure?" Holger whispered to her in the dark. "I can't ask you to leave your father and mother and your inheritance to take a chance on a peasant boy who can never give you what Nels could give you. Remember, those who go to America see their families for the very last time. Think carefully."

"I have counted the cost," Rosa replied. "Having love *is* wealth. Without it I am nothing. For ten years I have loved you and waited for you. Every hour of every day I have dreamed of the day we could be one. I will never love another. You are my family! My life! My love!"

In the darkness, her sweet, warm body next to his, his arms engulfing her, he had his answer. Nothing could part them.

"Rooosssaa! Rooosssaa!"

"Then we tell him right now."

"Yes, yes!" Holger could feel her heart beating wildly against his breast.

It seemed like yesterday.

Rosa's mother stood in the shadows, weeping. Hans had made all the arrangements. He had even spoken to the parish priest. The wedding would be a week from Sunday.

"You promised! You promised me to Holger!" Rosa sobbed. "I will not marry Nels. I can never love anyone but Holger. Tonight we have decided to go to America. There we will have more land than Nels or you!"

"Those who go to America never return," her mother wept. "Rosa, we can't stand against your father."

"No one will take my daughter to America!" Hans bellowed. "Get out, Holger! You must never see Rosa again. Go to America and forget her. The wedding is set! Rosa will do as I say. Someday she will thank me for not letting her marry a bungling peasant boy without land."

Like a bull moose, Hans steered Rosa toward the house. Holger heard him bang the prison door shut and lock it. All night he heard Rosa plead. All night he heard her Papa shout and her Mama cry. Holger pounded on the door and called to them. Grabbing his hunting rifle, Hans summoned the constable and ordered Holger off his land.

In the morning, when there was little hope, Holger went to see the parish priest. Surely he could talk sense to Rosa's parents.

"You do not bite the hand that feeds you," the priest told him.

"You mean you would sell Rosa's happiness for the measly offering her father puts in the collection plate?" Holger exploded.

"Who knows God's will for another? All I know is God's will for myself, and it is God's will that I don't get involved."

"I thought a preacher's only purpose *was* to get involved in this hurting world," Papa muttered when he realized his visit was futile.

Holger found it hard to search for a God who did not play fair. The best man did not always win. It was a fairy tale to believe that all things work together for good. If they did just this once, he might believe in God. That day Papa did not wonder why people turned their backs on the church.

How could you let that repulsive, lazy Nels have Rosa? Holger demanded of God. Finally, he accepted the bitter truth that young men who were not born to *herre gård* manors can never hope to become landowners in Denmark. God had nothing to do with it. Her father's worthless promise had been a carrot held out on a hopelessly long stick.

That night, overcome with the bitterest pain of his life, Holger made a pledge that went with him to the grave. He vowed that he would be a promise keeper.

He was able to slip Rosa a letter on Sunday as she passed his pew, her head bent in sorrow. He closed his ears as the preacher bellowed about God's mercy and love.

My beautiful Rosa, I cannot live without you. I am going to America. Come with me. I have enough money for two tickets. There we can be free. There we will have no high or low class. There rich and poor are equal and land is free for the taking. If there is a God, he is looking down on us and nothing is impossible with him. With all my heart, I am trying to find him. Right now he seems so endlessly far away. Only my love for you is real! Meet me by the mill pond at nine.

Rosa's father, however, intercepted the letter and came roaring to Holger after church. "You dumb peasant. No daughter of mine will throw away her life on a mere peasant. The wedding date is set and next week Rosa will marry Nels. Didn't you hear the preacher announce it in church today?"

Rosa had one of the hired men leave her little steamer trunk in the orchard for Holger. When he opened it he found a tear-stained letter.

> Father says I must marry Nels. It is best I do so. I dare not disobey. I will always love you and will carry you in my heart forever and ever until death. Another man may have my body, but you will always have my heart. Keep searching for God. He must be somewhere. *Farvel Jeg elsker dig for evighed* (Good-bye, I love you until eternity). Your obedient servant, Rosa.

So Holger left for America on the day the wedding bells rang for Rosa and Nels. It was time for action. He must not think of Rosa. That part of his life was over. One did not cross the mighty Atlantic and expect to return. With predictable foresight he had enlisted his brother Axel to accompany him. Having Axel with him would make it easier to forget Rosa, to feel some ties to family. They were two young, strong Danes, with new lives before them. Yes, he would forget Rosa. The great ocean must be a sea of forgetfulness.

Lonely and unbearably despondent, Holger stood on the deck straining to glimpse the last bit of sunlight on his fatherland—and his dreams. He soon lost sight of Denmark. With his last bitter-sweet look at the fertile land he loved and the land which had cost him Rosa, he decided Denmark had failed him. God had failed him.

Many of those leaving the old country brought on board balls of yarn, leaving one end of the line with someone on land. As the ship slowly cleared the dock, the balls unwound amid farewell shouts, fluttering handkerchiefs, and infants held high. After the yarn ran out, the long strips remained airborne, sustained by the wind, long after those on land and those at sea lost sight of each other.

Soon a great pea soup fog enveloped the ship and Holger could not even see the ocean. He turned to go down to his bunk when a great jolt nearly threw him overboard. In the fog the ship had hit a boulder! Water was pouring in. The ship was sinking! Folks were screaming hysterically! "Man the lifeboats! Full steam ahead to Norway!"

The crew and every able-bodied man struggled to help children and women into lifeboats, having barely enough time to jump to safety themselves. Terrified, in a tiny boat bouncing along behind the limping vessel headed for Norway, Holger mar-veled that his thoughts were not of the close call with death. So many were screaming that they would die in the cold and salty North Sea. Would that be so awful?

So near and yet so far! he thought. *Where is Rosa now? Oh God, take care of my tiny frail rose-bud with the dancing blue eyes, the golden hair and the ruby red lips which should have been*

*mine. Oh, God, how could you have let hulking
Nels with the bad temper and the unearned inheritance have Rosa? God, if there is a God, let me
find you, but until then, take care of Rosa. What
is life without Rosa?*

After a night in the murky salt brine, the boat
was safely anchored in Bergen. His only thought
was, "Oh God, so close to Rosa!" A second chance.
Maybe he could still make her change her mind.
He would go back and force her to leave Nels and
come to America with him.

No, he was dreaming, grasping at straws. Fate
had played cruel tricks on him. Rosa now belonged
to another. He must force his mind and heart to
turn westward across the vast Atlantic where the
Statue of Liberty opened its arms to the poor,
tired, huddled masses yearning to breathe free. He
would go west to the endless prairie to a land of
dreams and a chance to hope again. Perhaps there
he could discover God and find some meaning in
his despair.

There would be a week's delay in Norway while
the great seagoing vessel's hull was repaired. Everyone was told they could go ashore. First class
left first. Holger was fourth class—steerage.
Standing on the deck, he watched each passenger.
Why were they turning their faces westward, leaving family, fatherland, friends? Had the old country also failed them miserably? Young families
clutched their children. An old man said he
wanted nothing more than to see his grandchildren in America before he died. Some single
women were going to meet their lovers, and there

were some newlyweds who thought love would conquer all. Holger knew better.

He would have one week in Bergen, a respite, a time to sort out the pain, to heal and to plan a new strategy for America. He still had the money he had saved for the land. It had not been enough for land in Denmark but would perhaps buy him a whole *herre gård* in America.

It was a healing week, a time to discover the fjords, the fish market, the brilliant flower markets, to smell the sea and to try to forget all he had left behind.

While his brother flirted with the young ladies from the ship, Holger sought solitude by wandering alone in the harbor town. His heart seemed to be drawn to the flower market, especially to the roses. Here somehow he found a peace, a kind of beauty he had seen in Rosa, a bittersweet tranquility.

Chapter Three

A Rose for First Class

*P*erhaps it was his loneliness that made him notice Else. He had helped her into a lifeboat the night before and had seen her leave with the first class passengers this morning. Now he saw her alone at the flower market examining the flaming scarlet roses, enraptured with their dew-laden morning freshness. He remembered the roses that had grown long ago in his mother's kitchen garden. The roses were something famil-iar in an unfamiliar land, a bit of home. Roses al-ways smelled their same sweet best, no matter how dark the world might be. And morning was always fresh and new and the sun always came up, even in the middle of winter's wildest storms.

"*Dejlige* (gorgeous)," Holger ventured, almost surprised that he had spoken.

"*Ja, meget dejlige* (yes, very lovely)."

"*Vil du* (Would you like to have one)?"

She looked up in surprise, but Holger did not wait for her answer.

He passed the coin to the clerk and the scarlet rose to Else, the sparkling morning dew clinging to every sweet-scented petal. He reached over and briefly her outstretched hand touched his. It was soft and warm and reached into his utter loneliness.

A rose. A simple rose! An ocean to be crossed. Land to be found. Memories to be forgotten.

They walked quietly back to the ship, she to first class, he to fourth. They talked of the near tragedy of last night. It was best to put it out of one's mind. In a week they would have to trust the vessel to convey them across the Atlantic. Better to make small chitchat. So they talked of the rose. the morning. America. They laughed at the sea gulls swooping to snatch entrails thrown by ruddy Norsemen as they cleaned the morning's abundant raid on the windswept North Sea. Holger and Else walked in silence past the fish market where hawkers were shouting their wares: "*Frisk Fisk.* Nice fresh herring, yust caught this morning."

"Where are you going in America?" Holger asked in Danish, more to hear the familiar tongue than because he cared. Who mattered to him but Rosa? Never would he risk caring like that again.

"I have a brother in Omaha. Where are you going?"

"To Nebraska. My brother has heard of a Danish college at Blair where one can study agriculture free in exchange for working part time on a farm. Then we two brothers plan to work on farms until we can buy land. Land is all that matters. Without land one is nothing!"

"Land?" Else retorted. "Land is for peasants to farm and for land owners to rule. Some work with their brains, others with their brawn! In America there is much wealth and those who use their heads can get rich, richer than a king. That is what I intend to do in America."

Holger looked at the stranger in amazement. How had she come to that worldly conclusion so early in life? She must be all of nineteen. She was a Fenger, he learned. Her great-granduncle had for most of his life been *Kongens Præst,* priest to the king of Denmark.

"In fact," she boldly affirmed, "my great-granduncle confirmed the present king of Denmark."

Holger thought she looked like a little girl on a wild adventure. He marveled that she was traveling alone. He learned that she had quarreled with her family, and like the prodigal son in Jesus' parable was certain that the far country and an inheritance were all she needed.

He didn't ask for more information, but she needed to air her troubles and volunteered it. Her father was a wealthy *Godsejer* (manor owner) with dozens of hired servants. He had the absurd notion that all his children should learn to work. "If you need it, it will be good for you," he explained. "If you don't, it won't do any harm."

So he insisted all fourteen of his children learn to do all the work his servants did—common servant's work: milking cows, harvesting, tending cattle, churning, knitting socks, spinning yarn. Else grudgingly obeyed, although all this was far beneath her social standing.

Then, she told Holger, one bone-chilling winter day her father came to her with the absurd announcement that he had found her a job as a common servant on a neighboring *herre gård*.

With hurricane force Else had exploded: "ME? Work for common peasant wages? If you think I'd risk my reputation as a member of the landed gentry by scrubbing floors, waiting tables, and being a common maid for people of my own class, you've got another guess coming.

"No man of any worth would look at me, much less marry me, if I stooped to slave for mere wages. I know my heritage, and I will flee to America before I will be a servant!"

As Else confronted her father, she knew what cards were in her deck.

Else's mother had died in childbirth when Else was a toddler. An older sister, Anna, had lovingly given up marriage to raise the motherless family. In return, Papa had promised her the *gård*.

It had been a tough decision for her widowed father. Every oldest son in Denmark always inherited the manor. Nick was the oldest son. He knew his legal rights.

Enraged and fuming, with bitter words Nick confronted his widowed father, demanding the *gård* or his inheritance, NOW.

The words that had followed were caustic and stinging. Else's father cut Nick off from any inheritance at all. With one fatal expletive, Nick denounced his father, burned all his bridges behind him, and closed forever the door to his family. He announced he was going to America.

In frustration, Else's father, still deep in grief, countered his angry son with five acid words that he lived to regret moment by moment, hour by hour, day by day, until the day he met his Maker. They were, "I HOPE THE SHIP SINKS!"

For all the long and remorseful eternity that followed Nick's departure, Else's father mourned in deepest anguish the loss of his oldest son. He never heard from Nick again!

And now he was about to lose Else, too.

Else knew the story of her brother's angry departure all too well. Daily she had heard her Christian father pray for forgiveness. She had seen him grow old waiting for word from Nick, who had built a wall around himself as broad as the boundless Atlantic and as high as the star-spangled heavens above.

So Else played her best card. "I suppose," she shouted at her father, "I will be the second one you will send off to America without any inheritance. Are you sure you can live and die with that?"

Tragedy had mellowed her father, but he also knew his options were few. If he relented and gave Else her wish, it would divide the rest of the family. Those who stayed at home, worked on the manor, and waited for their inheritance would resent Else's receiving hers so easily; others already were piqued that Nick had gotten none. Either way, their family was hopelessly divided.

"I'll tell you one thing I told my Papa," Else boasted to Holger as she continued her story, "I told him that in America nobody will ever degrade me to scrub another floor or milk another cow. I'm done being treated like a peasant. In America they will know that I'm a Fenger, that Fengers are first class, and that nobility and peasants are cut from entirely different pieces of cloth."

Holger stared in disbelief at this stately young woman, so feminine looking and so indomitable and intrepid in spirit.

"It worked," Else confided in Holger. "I've got my inheritance sewn in right here." With astonishing boldness she patted her ample bosom.

Holger looked at her, speechless. *How very, very little there is that money can really buy,* he observed. *Being Danes is ALL we two have in common.*

How gladly, he thought bitterly, *would I have stayed with Rosa and worked as a peasant all my life for no other reward than to wake up each morning to the sunshine of her contagious smile. That would have been first class enough for both of us forever.*

Else's older sister Johanna had wept when Else left. Johanna was the peacemaker, a gentle dynamic nurse who had given up marriage to turn Danish insane asylums into mental hospitals which would become a pattern for the entire world. One of Else's brothers had developed the Danish Folk High Schools which pioneered quality education for youth. Fengers were nobility, distantly related to royalty. Else had always known that the

Fenger name opened all the right doors . . . now America's golden door was swinging wide for her.

Else's reasoning, however, seemed sheer nonsense to Holger. Give up a family willingly and forever over just money and good honest work! How senseless!

Holger had lost Rosa for lack of money, but not without fighting gallantly for ten long years to win her. With his inheritance he could have had her. Had he given up too easily? Why had he not stormed hell and demanded that Rosa come with him to America?

Suddenly Holger hated position, power, money, and conflict. Everything Else said was important was an enemy that had separated him from Rosa. Ironically, land and money had cost them both the same thing—family.

Holger wondered if anyone in America cared from which class you came. He had heard that there no one knew if you were a peasant or born in a palace. Would anyone even know the name Fenger? In America, those things families of nobility had worked generations to obtain seemed mysteriously to disappear once they stepped off Ellis Island. In America, you became simply one of the huddled masses yearning to breathe free. Nobody cared what class you were! And in America everyone worked!

"*Ak Ja*," Else declared. "Maybe ve vill show them." If she felt any fear it was well camouflaged.

She had written her older brother, Nick, whom she could not remember. Else had not been so dumb as he. She had demanded her money and gotten it. Now with money and the Fenger name, the future lay warm and inviting before her. She was traveling first class and she would be first class in America. She would marry first class! Live first class! Die first class! Money was the key to the shining future which lay just beyond the sun sinking in the golden west. Wait and see!

The next morning Else rose early, drawn by the sights and sounds of the harbor market and the fishing vessels home from sea, bouncing in carefree abandon in the bay. She had not returned to search for the handsome stranger from fourth class. No, he was but another ship passing in the night. She would never be fourth class. She would see to that.

But they did meet again, just as the day before. Holger had left the ship to see the sights and get fresh air. Fourth class was called steerage because it was located in the bowels of the ship next to the noisy engines. With neither breathing space below nor deck room above, hundreds and hundreds of steerage passengers were herded together like cattle. A walk on the deck when weather was good was an absolute necessity, for it was impossible to breathe clean air below in rough weather when the hatches were down. Neither cleanliness, decency, nor comfort were possible in fourth class. Yes, Holger was glad to get out of steerage for a few hours.

He headed for the flower market. There was Else again. She was examining a red rose and he was looking across the roses laughing at her. She, who was elegantly traveling first class, found they did have something in common . . . a fragrant, dew-covered scarlet rose.

Holger was thinking out loud when he said, "If I ever have a daughter as pretty as this rose, I'll call her Rose."

He bought Else another rose. It was just one *kroner* and it was worth it to banter with someone in Danish. He should have saved his money for land, but this was just one *kroner*. Maybe it would ease the pain and help him forget Rosa. Rosa, whose body now belonged to that bungling, roaring Nels who had nothing going for him but land and being born first class. Holger remembered that Rosa had said her heart would always belong to him. He hated first class and yet he had just bought a rose for a first class lady.

She held the rose in her hand as they walked silently. They could have heard little had they been speaking. Dock hands were straining their lungs screaming orders, dogs were barking, a *pølse* vender was hawking fat sausages *med alt* (with everything).

Maybe it was the pungent aroma of the sizzling fat sausages. Maybe it was the wonderful fresh salt air after a night in steerage. Maybe it was the piercing, wretched loneliness that made him spend another two *kroner* he should have saved for land on sausage. Perhaps Holger just enjoyed seeing a Danish girl laugh because the laughter would let him forget for a moment. When the sausages were devoured with gusto Holger thought with chagrin, *How dumb can a man be to spend money on first class. It is first class that lost Rosa.*

The spicy sausages on freshly baked crusty rolls, the great adventure ahead, the sound of Else's laughter. Perhaps it was worth two *kroner*. It was a beginning and he needed a new beginning.

When they were back on ship, Else went to first class, and he did not follow her. Fourth class was not allowed to go up to first class.

Holger was standing on deck at the rail, watching the sun sink in the golden west, when he looked up. There stood Else beside him. He had forgotten that although fourth class couldn't go up, first class can always step down. Even here on the ship bound for America, the land of the free, things had not changed much.

"Red sky at night, sailor's delight," Else laughed.

"Red sky in the morning, sailors take warning," he jested.

"Yes, but this is sunset."

They laughed together, and it felt good. The great ball of fire sank majestically into the unending ocean. The sky turned black except for a lone star on which each made a secret wish. Then she turned to go back upstairs where the elusive barrier of class separated them.

Maybe in America there will be upward mobility for the peasant. Maybe, he thought for the first time, *when I have money, I can find another Rosa.* But did he want another? Something strange had stirred in him. Something he thought was dead when he first lost Rosa.

In the tranquil beauty of the new adventure, he felt he had betrayed Rosa when he found himself wondering if another could fill the empty space.

The next days in fourth class passed slowly. He survived for ten days with smelly food and atmosphere so thick and dense with smoke and body odors that many got seasick even when the waters were calm. When a Northeasterner whipped the roaring Atlantic, everyone became desperately sick. Then there was head lice and terrible scratching! Bunks were burlap-covered bags of straw or seaweed and the life preserver served double duty as a pillow. Food was served in 25-gallon tanks and each passenger ate from his or her own tin mess kit.

Fourth class was filled with Jewish war orphans, Armenians who had witnessed killing and torture at the hands of the Turks, Irish people who had nearly starved to death, and Russians fleeing persecution who had seen so much torture and privation before they decided to come to America that now all that carried them was the dream. Everything would be so rich and wonderful in America, they all believed, that pain, hardship and even the sting of lifelong separation could be endured.

Listening to the other passengers' stories, Holger's own pain eased. On nights when the sea was still he would take out his flute and invite others who had hidden harmonicas and accordions in the luggage to join him. For a brief evening there would be dancing and singing. Always there were long discussions about America.

Many acquaintances were made within each ethnic group, and some of these friendships lasted a lifetime. Many immigrants chose destinations in the new land near others who spoke their mother tongue, where they could stay close to the new friends they had made aboard ship. Scandinavians often went to Minnesota for farming; Slavic groups tended to go to the mines, steel mills, and slaughter houses; Jews went to New York and the needle trades. Each sought out a place where the familiar language offered a bit of home on foreign soil.

Chapter Four

The Lady with the Lamp

*H*olger was on deck at sunrise feeding the sea gulls which had followed the ship across the ocean when he first sighted the lady with the lamp standing tall in New York harbor. Everyone clapped and cheered when they saw the statue because now they were really in America. One weary mother said, "*Ach Ja.* I am glad she is a voman. She vill understand a voman's pain."

The thrill was unbelievable, but in the back of everyone's mind was the fear of being sent back at Ellis Island. Twenty percent of those who came to America were denied entrance. Everyone on the ship was terrified at this possibility.

Yes, it this is real, Holger thought. He really had left Denmark behind forever—Rosa and the land and his dreams.

Everywhere there was chaos. People were pushing . . . shoving . . . shouting, in Norwegian, German, Danish, or broken English.

Holger stayed with his brother Axel and they were processed together. Another brother, Gunnar, had come over earlier. On the boat Gunnar had met a friend who was going to Wisconsin, a place with cheese factories and hundreds of Holstein cattle. The cows stood waist high all summer in lush green meadows, their heavy udders bulging with rich, golden cream. In Wisconsin, the story went, farmers soon became millionaires without even trying. That is where Gunnar lived and prospered and where he died.

Holger and Axel soon gladly forgot the difficult ten-day journey in steerage. There were passports to examine, luggage to check, physical examinations to be made. Else, too, was soon forgotten.

Jostling in line, fourth class passengers were the last to be processed. Before these passengers were taken on board in Denmark they had been given antiseptic baths, had their baggage fumigated, and were examined by company doctors. Now they had to endure extra physical exams and shots, and each person was stripped and searched.

Each newcomer had his or her own reasons for coming, a set of personal goals that made the risky voyage worth taking. These dreams and ambitions were nurtured by tales of gold on the streets, free land, and a single Texan who owned more cattle than lived in the entire Balkans.

But there were also stories of reality in America. An old Italian tale told of the man who said, "I came to America because I heard the streets were paved with gold. When I got here, I found out three things: first, the streets weren't paved with gold; second, they weren't paved at all; and third, I was expected to pave them."*

Holger had briefly seen Else on the ferry going to New York City. She had slipped him her brother's address in Omaha written in a tiny, engraved card with a rose etched under her name. Smelling faintly of verbena, the note said she was going to spend a week in New York seeing and doing the things she wanted to do with no family to tell her what first class ladies did or didn't do.

Holger tucked the card into his leather pouch in the steamer trunk Rosa had given him, along with his money, passport, and a picture of Rosa. He would never see Else again, but it would be good to think he knew at least one person besides his brothers in this immense land.

Holger knew one English word—"pie"—and he tried it out on the vender on the dock. The pie he bought had a crust on top, some apples in the middle and something much too hard to chew on the bottom. It tasted like paper. He tried a bite and threw it away. A man next to him eagerly picked it up and devoured it—minus the paper plate. Holger was laughed at for the first time for being a dumb foreigner.

He realized he had a lot to learn.

---

* Chermyell, Wasserman, Shapiro, *Ellis Island, A History of Immigrant Experience,* (New York: Macmillan Publishing Co. Inc.).

That had been ten years ago. He had learned a lot about America since then. He had gone to Dana College for a year, then to Ames, Iowa, where young Danish farmers who wanted to learn butter and cheese making, and raising hogs, cattle and crops, could get free tuition in return for apprenticeship.

He and Axel were soon working on a farm three times the size of the land that had claimed his Rosa. Young and eager to learn, they worked from early morning until late at night, then burned the midnight oil to study. Soon they were up again and out into the fields and immaculate barns. They fell into bed at night hardly able to remember more than that their bone-weary limbs must rest so they could get up before the sun's first rays again crept across the endless prairie.

It was good to be this tired! Holger could forget about Denmark and Rosa . . . except on starry nights when he looked up into the sky and thought, *This is the only thing which is exactly like Denmark. That same golden moon is shining down on Rosa, sleeping with that rich and unfeeling Nels, bearing his children, sitting in his paid pew on Sunday . . . and all because of land.* Ironically Holger was working for exactly the same despicable demons—money and land—that had stolen Rosa from him.

Funny how he could hardly picture Rosa in his mind. He still had her picture locked in the steamer trunk's secret compartment. The little note Else had given him in New York, the one with the rose on it, was tucked away there also.

One lonely night in Iowa he took the picture of Rosa out of its hiding place. The engraved card with the rose on it fell out, too. Holger walked to the college mercantile and bought a penny postcard with a picture of a beagle with drooping ears howling pathetically at the full moon. It read, "I'm lonesome without you." In a moment of impulse he addressed it to Else. After it slipped irretrievably into the mail box he felt chagrined that he might have set himself up for another war between first and fourth class.

After arriving in America, Else had spent her week in New York and then embarked on a monstrous black puffing dragon of a passenger train to cross a land so wide and empty it could swallow Denmark ten times over. She was headed for Omaha and her brother Nick.

Nick's dreams of wealth and prosperity had ended in a small cleaning establishment where he sweat fifteen hours a day trying to make ends meet. Nick, who as the oldest son should have inherited the Danish *herre gård,* never forgave his father.

Life had dealt Nick a bitter blow. Resentful and sullen, he bit back at his sons, his wife, and the unfair world which had deceived him into giving up his inheritance without a battle. If he had only known how to fight. If only! If only! Later, he abandoned his wife. He died a penniless alcoholic loner in a land of wealth and broken dreams.

Else stayed with them for two weeks. Then she got a room and an English tutor at the Y.W.C.A. Every day she went to school with Nick's five-year-old son. She spent a few days in each grade and finally took a nurse's aide position at the hospital to try to learn more English.

When Else had learned enough to get along, the head nurse suggested she enter nurses' training. She worked and studied long hours. With no time or place to spend her inheritance, she banked it and lived on the eight dollars a month training pay. Two years later, R.N. in hand, just as she was headed to New York and fame and fortune, my father's card came. It was dog-eared and had been in the mail for many weeks.

"I was glad to hear from you," she wrote, "I am coming through Iowa on my way to New York."

He met her at the depot and showed her the prodigious farm where he worked. It was larger than her father's *herre gård* back home. The corn was more lush and the cattle fatter. The sleek lean porkers were scientifically grown for the great Chicago packing houses.

It had been two horrendously busy years and work, distance, and loneliness had dimmed Rosa's image. Holger painted a young man's dreams as he talked to Else. Soon he would own twice as much land as both their parents had owned back in the old country.

Holger found the courage to suggest that they meet again. She gave him her address and waved to him as the train pulled out.

Two years in America had taught Else many things besides the English which she spoke haltingly. Here social class meant nothing! In her tiny garret in the sweltering heat of summer and the bitter biting cold of winter she longed for the family she had left so hastily.

She hesitated to admit, even to herself, that she was unbearably lonely. The only Danish she heard was in the Lutheran church on Sundays when she could sometimes get off duty long enough to sing the Gruntvig hymns and hear scripture read in a tongue so melodic and overpowering that she sat weeping for the meadowlarks singing in the poplars and aspens of her homeland. She had learned that the Fenger name meant little in America. Money mattered greatly. But money did not assuage loneliness.

By the time she had saved $1,000 from her wages she heard from Holger.

"*Er du gift?* (Are you married?) *Er du enesome?* (Are you lonely?)"

The answer was "no" and "yes." She bought a train ticket to Iowa.

It was not the wedding Else would have had if she had married first class in Denmark. If she dreamed of a long white gown and the magnificent church of her great-granduncle, she did not voice the thought. On a spring morning, buds bursting after a rain, two lonely immigrants quelled their longing for the fatherland and friends. They found a Lutheran church and a minister whose redeeming quality was that he could say the sacred vows in the mother tongue. Axel and his new bride, Nina, were the only attendants.

America had taught them much about reality. It was too big, too strange, too impersonal to conquer alone.

Holger and Axel had finished their formal schooling and secured good jobs on the farms where they had been working. They were promised the opportunity to buy land when they finished the three years left on their apprenticeships.

By the time the three years ended, Mama and Papa had two children. The rich, black Iowa loam was going up in price—a whole sixty dollars an acre. They invested in a 200-acre farm that was priced sky-high.

Uncle Axel was content with his new Danish wife. They were adamant that they would buy land there and never leave Iowa. They never did. They lived and died in Iowa, raised an American family and found the American dream despite the Great Depression.

Then Else heard about Askov, Minnesota, where everyone spoke Danish. A distant relative, Dr. Palmer Nathaniel Fenger, lived there. A physician, he had gone to this pioneer Danish settlement with a sincere desire to pour his life into something bigger than himself.

Else wrote to the Danish Folk Committee which had decided to sponsor a colonization project for Danes. They flooded her with brochures that read:

> Those who search for a bit of Denmark in America need search no more. We can supply half-price tickets on the train to this marvelous land of opportunity. The grassy meadows filled with red clover lend themselves to the creamery and dairy business.

There are trains just 75 miles from the big cities which boast 400,000 citizens just waiting for your produce.

Strawberries, raspberries, cucumbers, onions and cabbage, milk, butter and eggs can be sent to Chicago or the big Eastern cities. Beautiful birch-laden forests, cheap land and cordial Danes beckon to you to a bit of Denmark, the land of promise, Askov, Minnesota.

Here folks would know she was a Fenger, that she came from nobility, that she was first class! Else had hoarded the $1,000 she had earned in New York. She also had a bit of her inheritance left which would go for cattle, hogs, and a house worthy of a Fenger. Here she could buy the position, land, and standing she missed. They could sell the Iowa land for a good price and get a much better bargain in Minnesota where land was only $17 an acre for good land, $14 for scrub.

They arrived in Askov on a Sunday morning just in time to hear the Lutheran Church bells ring. They rang exactly like in Denmark! Although they were only visiting, moving to Askov was a done deal . . . for Else. They stayed at the hotel called Danevirke. Late in the night Else could hear the young swains still singing Danish drinking songs.

Askov was host to the Danish Young People's *samfund* that weekend. The church was gloriously packed with immigrant young people from North and South Dakota and Wisconsin who reminded

Else of happy days in Denmark. A few even remembered the Fengers from Denmark.

Else had not expected to find such a resplendent Lutheran church in America. She could not know then that loneliness and desolation had built this house of God. Immigrants, desperately hungry for the old country and often feeling far from God, had gone without bread or shoes to make this glorious replica of the true Denmark their lasting heritage on American soil.

Tall tapers flickered in the stately brass candelabra and a marvelous bell rang in the tall white steeple. The organ blended with the voices of Danish immigrants bonded together in a strange land singing "*Dejlig er Jorden*" (Beautiful Savior, Lord of Creation). The liturgy and Lord's prayer were painfully reminiscent of all they had left in a land far across the endless sea.

After worship there was a potluck *selskab* fellowship where people who already had bought and settled there painted Askov in terms only those bitterly hungry for fellowship could have used. The table groaned with *æblekage, rullepølse,* and Danish meatballs served with lots of steaming black coffee. It seemed a land of plenty—of all Else needed.

Their hosts were not dishonest. They talked of the plenteous blueberries, of the summer picnics and the wonderful Danish church with the towering steeple and magnificent chimes. They took pains to point out the outstanding consolidated grade school, one of the very first in America. Children were transported to school by sled or wagon.

Both English and Danish were taught there; no teacher was hired who was not fluent in writing, reading, and speaking Danish.

Yes, here families pulled together, worked together. Just look at this magnificent church. Here they were really community in this strange, new country. "A bit of our homeland on foreign soil," they boasted.

Holger protested that he had an offer to work for an Iowa farmer who raised 100 bushels of corn an acre. With the extra money from that job, very soon he could begin to buy more rich, fertile Iowa land, land just as good as in the old country. Maybe it was more expensive, but "if you pay peanuts you get monkeys," he argued.

True, around Askov the virgin forest was in its primeval glory. White and Norway pines towered to the skies. But transportation was largely by foot. There were few roads and they were primitive. Brush covered much of the territory. Only when the stumps were blasted and the stones piled together could you farm. He heard stories of drought and grasshoppers and hail. Mama heard of the abundance of wild blueberries—you could pick a bucketful in just an hour. They told her of the rutabaga crop which one visionary Dane was sure would make Askov nationally famous. She thought to herself, *I have the $1,000 dollars and some inheritance for down payment.*

Else and Holger attended the Sunday night folk dancing at the new Danish Brotherhood hall. Because she was heavy with child, Else watched with envy as young folks danced away the night as if they had not a care in the world. She dreamt of being young again, of Papa swinging her around and around on the dance floor as young lads had done a few years ago in another world. Perhaps they could capture something here which seemed missing.

And so on a dewy spring morning, just as the first yellow-tipped meadowlarks were returning and the jubilant Danish bells pealed for morning worship, when longing for the homeland crowded out good common sense, an artful, subtle land broker sold Mama and Papa forty acres of land. Those forty acres would defiantly resist both plow and planter and would soon bankrupt my Papa and Mama of their youth, vigor, and dreams.

True, gold did not grow on trees in America. But with that many Danes and Dr. Fenger here, and the church bells ringing, and the robins returning, it seemed to Mama that she was back home again in the world she once wanted desperately to leave behind forever.

They went back to Iowa to pack up their belongings and arrived in Askov on a sunshiny summer day with two small girls in tow and another child on the way. They had little else but youthful hope and strong backs. They would need both in the days ahead.

Dr. Fenger met them at the train station. Yes, this was exactly like Denmark, except that here one could own his very own *gård*. Better yet, here was a Fenger. Dr. Fenger had become the undisputed civic leader in the community, not by force or education or position, but by a deep sense of service to his God and this group of Danish adventurers. Because of his great humanitarian service to Askov, some folks here even remembered that the Fengers had helped to make Denmark a world leader in medicine, agriculture, religion, and education. Being a Fenger meant something here.

Mama soon learned, though, that it was not being born first class that made Dr. Fenger first class. He was a typical old-fashioned country doctor, intensely interested in the welfare of the individual. He made calls on foot, sometimes in bitter cold and raging snowstorms. He never turned down a call in order to spare himself. He had no standard rates, and was not interested in what payment he could collect. Too often he let the bill slide. When the larder was in dire straits, Mrs. Fenger took steps to collect enough to keep body and soul together.

There was no dentist in Askov, so he pulled teeth. No veterinarian, so he saved many a farmer from disaster. He delivered hundreds of babies, and wore his body out digging his car out of mud and snow and sleet. Some said he was too old-fashioned, lacked bedside manners, and didn't show enough sympathy unless you were really ill. But he never lost a patient through carelessness and he never sought glory or wealth for himself. Yet he enriched the world. He died young, the gigantic hero of all of us.

His house was filled with music—classical and contemporary, secular and sacred. Once a month everyone was invited to his house for "music appreciation night." As Mrs. Fenger played majestic

Bach, Beethoven, and Mozart, Else marveled that Mrs. Fenger easily could have played in the great concert houses of Europe. Instead she had chosen to bury herself and her enormous talents on the rim of the windswept prairie, investing everything in the love of a man who would not even collect his bills.

If the northern lights were more spectacular than usual, Dr. Fenger and his wife would walk lovingly arm-in-arm through Askov, going door to door calling attention to them.

Three years later, Mama's money and what Papa had been able to save had been spent on a four-room house, three sturdy work horses, a plow, seed, a windmill, six brown Jersey milk cows, 100 Rhode Island Red chickens, and a brood sow.

So far they had been able to clear just 20 acres of the unyielding prairie sod. It was 1918 and Ford cars were rolling off the assembly line. Thousands in Detroit had jobs, earning a whole four dollars a day. It was easy to borrow money to build a barn.

The first winter wheat crop had come up during an Indian summer autumn. Then it had been covered with six feet of snow in a Minnesota blizzard. They had weathered the storm, risking life and limb to get to the barn to milk each morning. Fence posts were covered with snow until spring and no one could tell where the roads had been. But they felt secure because they knew that the winter wheat lay hidden safely under the blanket of white. They dreamed of springtime, of the lush green blades raising their heads during the first early thaw of March. They imagined the crop waving tall and luxurious and heading into burnished golden wheat to sell to the Chicago market and to feed the sleek porkers fattening in the barn. Yes, all they needed now was good spring rain and God's eternal sunshine.

But April slipped into June as each day the farmers searched the unyielding clouds for signs of rain. The vesper bells rang from the church steeple. The parish pastor prayed for rain. The nubbins of lush green winter wheat turned to wilted, crackly stalks fit for little more than to let the pigs root for forage.

Holger tried to pray but he did not know how to address a God who would play such games. The demons from hell that had stolen Rosa must be at work here, too. Else counted the $16 they received for the crop that year and longed for just one glimpse of the land across the sea.

By July something was wrong with the milk cows. One cow dropped its calf. Some calves which were born alive had huge deformed goiters, were scrawny and brought next to nothing at market. Dr. Fenger told them to put iodine in the water to cure the goiter. He even suggested doing the same for humans, but that was considered *nar* (pure foolishness). Water was water.

The next year's crop gave hope. The rye and wheat provided money to make the farm payment. The family—they had had four children in five years and another was on the way—had weathered that winter and planted in hope. They were young and strong and believed they would make it. But that was before the grasshoppers blackened the skies, harvesting every single blade of green before marching on to the next field. When Holger realized they had carefully planted their abhorrent eggs after their invasion, he lost hope for next year's crop.

Four years after arriving in Askov, all Holger had to show was the stumps and stones dug out of the barren ground, a few scrawny milk cows, a flock of Rhode Island Red chickens, a loudmouthed rooster, and six mouths to feed.

Somewhere in the distance, beyond the stone fence which separated the fields, the old fifty-niner mail train was steaming into town. Folks would be gathered around the general store hoping for bits of news from Denmark. Long ago Holger had burned his bridges. Someone who came back from visiting in Denmark had slipped him a note from Rosa, who was carrying her seventh child. The note read, "I should have come with you. I'm so lonesome without you but it is best we forget. It can never be now."

Well, life had not been easy for him, either. Just yesterday he had experienced the blinding pain of a toothache. With no dentist in the region and no money for a dentist anyway, he had taken a pair of pliers and pulled the demon himself. *Man kan hvad man vil.* You can do what you will— what you have to do!

In the recesses of his heart he still cherished Rosa, but he also dearly loved Else, differently per-haps, but he loved her deeply and felt responsible that life had not been easier for her.

Where was God when you needed him?

Chapter Five

Come Quickly!
It Is Time!

*T*he land—the terrible, stubborn land—had separated Holger from Rosa. But it had also betrayed Else's dreams. Holger felt ashamed that she cooked potato soup night after night, hoping they would not run out of potatoes and that the cows would not dry up. Patiently she made Danish rye bread from the only crop they had been able to harvest last year.

Else, heavy with a fifth child, was out milking. She had lost a child the year before and had said she was glad. How would they have fed another mouth?

Holger, working in the fields, heard a shout. "Papa, Papa, come quickly!" He saw it was his oldest who came running full speed, her hair flying free in the summer wind.

"Hurry, *hurtigt!*" she was calling, half in English, half in Danish. "Mama says it is her time."

With lightning speed Holger unhooked the plow. In a flash he was back at the barn, threw the bridle on Daisy and was off, prodding her insistently to race her weary bones full speed to fetch Dr. Fenger.

As fast as the work-worn beast and poor roads would allow, Holger returned with the doctor. As they entered the room where Else was struggling to give birth, Holger looked at her with love and deepest compassion. All she had done since he married her was struggle.

After he was banished to the kitchen, Holger walked the floor waiting apprehensively for a healthy cry. Suddenly Else's cries of pain ended, but he heard no baby crying. Instead the stifling hot summer night was filled with an ominous silence.

When he finally heard a frail whisper of a whimper he realized something was dead wrong. Holger broke uninvited into the room. Yes, Else was no longer struggling . . . but the baby was fighting for every tiny breath.

"Goiter! It's the confounded goiter!" Dr. Fenger exploded as he handed the baby to Papa. "I told you pigheaded Danes what to do about goiter but nobody would listen! You thought I was old-fashioned? Well, now maybe you will listen when this beautiful little baby dies, a victim of your stupidity. First it is your cattle, now it is your children."

Papa was crushed. Mama replied stoically, "The baby will die and it is best. Doctor, when you go back to town, get the pastor. There is no time to lose. We must baptize her before she dies or she will never see the face of Jesus. Tell him he can take care of saying a prayer for her burying at the same time."

Papa's heart melted as he held the tiny slip of humanity, a rosebud struggling to open to the sun! She was a baby who could hardly breath, who could not cry or swallow. She was a baby he had to save. As truly as Papa had fallen in love with Rosa and Else, so he fell in love with this tiny struggling bit of life. No challenge in the past, no prayer in the present compared to this.

Holger wanted to cover his ears to his wife's grim predictions. He had to get outside where there was fresh air, where he could think of a solution. A great mellow moon was rising in splendor across the prairie. "I'm losing everything I touch, God . . . the crops, the cattle . . . and now I've killed this baby with my own stubbornness. God, send an answer!"

From across the meadow he heard a night owl hoot. Then as he listened, it sounded as if God were saying, "Iodine, iodine, iodine." Dr. Fenger had said it loud and clear to everyone in Askov: "All the Askov water lacks is iodine."

Now Holger no longer felt helpless. Even though he didn't know God, he was sure God had deigned to speak directly to him. Still clutching the baby fiercely, he went back inside and confronted the good doctor with his idea.

Dr. Fenger was ecstatic. God was answering his prayer. What he had not been able to accomplish with months of cajoling he saw he could prove if only they could keep the baby alive. For months he had carried the unsolicited bottle of iodine in his bag, waiting for just such a moment.

The country kitchen became his emergency room. Quickly he called for milk and sugar. Gentle as a woman, he mixed a formula. He showed Holger how to force the warm liquid through the baby's lips with a medicine dropper and how to hold the baby and rock to keep her from strangling on the milk.

Next he fixed warm iodine milk for Else. "Drink as much of this as you can," he ordered, "for as long as you nurse the baby."

"*Nar,*" Else responded. "We need a preacher, not a doctor performing experiments." But she drank the milk anyway.

After Dr. Fenger left, Papa wrapped the worn blanket tighter around his tiny bundle and rocked back and forth. *Drop! Breathe! Drop! Breathe! Clock, stop ticking! Give us time! Little canary, open your mouth. God, give us a miracle! Breathe! Breathe! Breathe!* Holger thought.

The pastor arrived at midnight. He took one look at the struggling baby, the tiny house on the barren prairie, and the six mouths to feed and comforted Else by saying, "You are right. It could be the will of God."

He donned his clerical cassock while Papa, still holding the baby in one strong arm, filled the old blue enamel wash basin for the baptism.

"What name do you give this child?"

"A name? She doesn't need one. Can't you see

she is going to die?" Else announced with resignation.

"She will have a name! No child God has sent into the world should be nameless," Holger said gently. "We will call her Rosa. No, dis is America; ve vill call her Rose." He was remembering a spring morning in a Bergen flower market, a young Danish girl with dreams and hopes, and a delicate rose bought for one *kroner* with the promise that if he ever had a daughter that beautiful her name would be rose.

"What difference does it make? She is going to die anyway," Else replied. Her dreams had been lost in the blizzards and droughts of her hard life.

"I baptize thee Rose Voetmann," the preacher intoned.

"No," Papa interrupted. "Call her Rose FENGER Voetmann. She must never forget that she is also a Fenger."

I survived. In a moment of bitterness for her lot, my mother once told me she had hoped I would not. There had been no money for another baby. Many folks were just plain starving. Mama had visited a neighbor who was cooking her cat. A dozen or more families, desolate as the land they had bought, had left Askov in bitterness and disillusionment.

But where could we go? If I had understood all these things better I might not have grown up feeling so unwanted.

When I was four, Dr. Fenger said many of the Askov children, including my brother and me, needed to have their tonsils removed. No one in

Askov had money for operations. Mama struck a
deal with the doctor and the church. If they could
use the church basement, if Dr. Fenger would re-
move our tonsils free of charge, Mama would serve
as his nurse without pay. Everyone else would
have to pay ten dollars a child. Later that deal
would haunt Mama, but at the time it seemed a
good barter.

As a four-year-old, I was petrified at what
seemed to me to be hundreds of children spitting
out blood as we lay on cots in the dark, dank
church basement. I was sure I was going to die and
I had never heard how to get to heaven.

I held Papa's hand and asked him about
heaven. "You won't die from tonsils," he said, but
he didn't laugh at my questions. He promised he'd
find answers for me. I prayed for an angel to come
to Papa and me and show us the way.

No sun shone in the damp church basement on
that dreary December day. Mama lit the kerosene
lamps on the wall. Then, clear as day, I saw an
angel. He had on a flowing snow-white monk's robe
anchored securely at the waist with a cord. Had
God heard me? I didn't dare dream that the angel
had come just for me.

All the other children were sick, too, but he
came straight to my cot. I felt a miraculous security when he reached for my trembling hand. Then
he reached for Papa's. It was the first time anyone had ever prayed out loud just for me. He asked
God to make me well, to make me a great blessing in the world. I was coming out of the ether and
it seemed to me he had wings. Papa told me it was

Pastor Rodholm but I knew the pastor did not have wings.

That night as I floated back into the peaceful world of sleep I learned a great spiritual truth which has given me a sense of assurance ever since. "For he will command his angels concerning you to guard you in all your ways" (Psalm 91:11). I didn't learn until much later that the angel had come because Papa had gone upstairs and talked with the pastor. He told him I was afraid I might die and asked him to come talk with me. Papa was like that.

From upstairs, I could hear the organist practicing the great old Danish hymns. The music seemed to float down from heaven. I felt an overwhelming security. God's house was sheltering me from the dark, foreboding world filled with hardship. His angels were in charge and Papa was beside me and cared even about my fears.

As the great organ swelled and the music drifted into my heart, I fell in love—hopelessly and incurably in love—with the church. It was a love that ecclesiastical blundering and bureaucratic rejection has never dimmed. This love was to last for a lifetime and strengthen me time and again.

In a harsh, cruel world of sharp-edged realities, the church was loving and tender. I felt encircled by her wooden arms.

Outside it was dark; a winter storm was howling. Let it storm! At that moment I felt closer to God than I had known was possible. What did it matter that Mama may not have wanted me, that we had no money, and that I was bleeding? God had a plan for my life and I would live to find it some day.

Prophetically, God was revealing a part of that plan to me that day. It involved the church and what it could do for those who were hurting and afraid and alone. Some day when I was grown, when I saw a room full of hurting people, I would be the one to pray, hug, and love away the hurt of the world. I would point them to heaven and God's church. I didn't know then that my love for the church would consume my whole life.

Late that night when I was back home and hurting, Papa wrapped me in an old comforter and pulled the ancient kitchen rocker next to the wood stove. I asked him about the feeling I had about falling in love with the church and about my search for God. Papa rocked me gently until the brief December sun came creeping across the horizon. As he rocked, he talked. Maybe he thought I was asleep. He seemed not to be talking to me at all but to a God he had not found.

The little house on the wide white prairie was quiet except for the moaning wind and the kitchen clock ticking away the night. Everyone else was asleep. Papa closed the door softly so we were alone. In a gentle, quiet voice, he called out to a God who seemed to have forgotten him: "*Herre Gud* (Lord God), if there is a God, where are you? I need help. The winter is so long, the nights are so deep, the spring rains are so uncertain, the pestilence is so persistent . . . Long, long ago in the gentle flat fields of Denmark, in the little thatched house where my Mama lived, you seemed to be in every song she ever sang, in every robin's warble, every whispering willow tree, every church bell that chimed across the countryside. Oh, God, I am so little and I am so tired of struggling and you are so big. But you are so far away. In this vast America I just can't find you. Oh, God, you must be somewhere out there. Please help. I can't go it alone."

Then, barely audible, he sobbed, "I've promised this little girl I'd find the answers for her, and I've got to keep my promises!" He stroked my hair as he held me tight. His great chest began heaving. I pretended to be asleep so Papa would not know I had heard him weeping uncontrollably.

For the first time in my life, I felt close to someone.

Oh, Papa, I thought, *you are so good. Maybe we can find God together.*

I was glad I had had my tonsils taken out. I was now bonded to my Papa. We were cut from the same cloth—fourth class, maybe, and often outsiders, but with that kind of love, we would find the answers to my questions about heaven. Papa would keep his promise! I just knew it.

After that night, I began tagging around after Papa wherever he went. Sometimes I rode the two-row cultivator. Sometimes I climbed the windmill with him all the way to the top where we could see the church way off in the distance. Soon I was up as early as Papa, milking cows every morning. I sensed that Papa and I were on a great adventure to find the answers and keep Papa's promises.

Chapter Six

Charlie Chaplin and I

*I*t wasn't very long before finding God was not just a luxury for me.

Folks in Askov had few pleasures during those meager days. The pastor had arranged for a free Charlie Chaplin movie to be shown at the Danish Brotherhood Lodge Hall.

Papa piled us all in the wagon and we went. With amazement and unbelief, we saw for the first time real people talking on the screen, doing somersaults and cavorting as if they were alive. It was a miracle. Whatever would they invent next? America was a wonderful country where even pictures could talk. We laughed all the way home.

It was all we talked about for days. My brothers and sisters all tried the somersaults, but I was too small and they wouldn't let me try. They said

I was the baby. That sent up a red flag and made me all the more determined to try. On Saturday night when everyone was out in the barn finishing the chores, I hurried to the house, climbed on a chair which served as a tightrope, and tried a flip.

Mama's big kettle of bath water was boiling furiously on the stove, ready to be poured into the wash tub where each of us in turn would take our Saturday night bath. Mama was first, then Papa, then all the other children. I, being the youngest, was last.

I was much too absorbed in being Charlie Chaplin to notice the kettle's long handle. As I attempted my flip, it caught my legs. A horrendous crash followed my somersault. Boiling water seared much of my body. The pain was so intense I screamed in agony.

Papa was just coming from the barn. Hearing my screams, he began to run. Much later that night, after much of my skin had been painfully removed along with my home-knit wool socks and long underwear, Dr. Fenger told Papa that I could possibly die. If I lived, I would probably never walk again.

Papa was undaunted. I suppose he tried to call to his unknown God. He had lost one Rosa and he was not about to lose this one. From scraps of wood he built a kiddie car, the forerunner of the modern tricycle, and defiantly set it in the middle of the kitchen. It was his symbol that one day I would be out of bed and walking. Was it his way of calling to his unknown God?

When Papa's faith was rewarded and I was finally able to sit up, he made me push myself around on the kiddie car for a whole year until I could walk again. God would not let me die or lose the use of my legs. When I was able to walk alone for the first time, Papa took me to town. We entered the sacred sanctuary of the Danish church, me hobbling on my newfound legs.

Papa wept great hulking sobs of relief. I knew I would never be alone with someone loving me as much as Papa did. He told me earnestly, "God has let you walk because he has a great plan for your life." I knew then that some day we would find God and when we did, nobody would ever have to search for him as hard as Papa and I were searching.

Often at night I listened to Mama and Papa through the thin walls. Hoover was saying that if people would just work harder there would be no depression. Mama, whose money was all gone, tended to agree with him, but I didn't. Papa worked harder than anyone could imagine. I did not know then how useful these lessons on poverty would be in years to come when God would call me to be a missionary.

I also learned much about strife and discord during those years. Some Askov people in the church were powerfully unhappy that our family had not had to pay the $10 for the tonsil operations. Others felt Mama acted as if she were much too first class. Whatever it was, Mama was not happy with Askov. She felt we had to move and she was doing something about it.

"This morning in church I heard them talking about a Danish community in Wisconsin called West Denmark. There are no stumps and stones there and the land is so rich you can get 100 bushels of corn to the acre," she told Papa.

"But where would we get the kind of money to buy land there?" Papa protested.

"It would be easy," Mama persisted. "You can buy 200 acres for $10,000 and you only have to put $500 down."

"Credit? Buy on credit? What pure foolishness! One hailstorm or one summer of grasshoppers would wipe us out and they would take the farm."

"Do what you please, but I'm NOT staying here. Folks just don't appreciate me here. They are all such peasants."

"Peasants, Mama? Nobody is a peasant who is loved as much as I love you. Oh, dear, dear Mama, don't you see that here in America we are all the same? We all have to struggle to build America and that makes us all equals. Cheer up! Besides, we have finally gotten the land cleared. See those fence rows of stumps and stones I've hauled out of the fields? Now we are just ready for our first really good crop. We are getting our mortgage nearly paid off. This is the first year we can really break even. Why leave it all now to get head over heels in debt and risk losing everything? No, Else, no! Please!"

But Mama left few options.

"Folks here aren't my kind," she explained. "I'm not going to stay where I'm not wanted. Since the land is cleared we could sell it for more than we paid for it and we can get more credit to buy in Wisconsin."

This made little sense to Papa. Nevertheless, it was decided we would move to the promised land even though by 1926 panic was sweeping America. The Ford Motor plant had shut down. Henry Ford had written much that was anti-Semitic. A man named Hitler was rising to power in Europe and was reading with gusto everything Mr. Ford wrote. Herbert Hoover was president and banks were shaky. Papa talked about a very rich man named J. P. Morgan who said, "A smart man makes his money with money. God wouldn't have made sheep if he didn't expect them to be sheared."

Papa was afraid that the thin veneer of American prosperity was covering a festering wound. He was mighty afraid of buying a farm on credit and thought times would get better where we were. The land finally was cleared and we could make it at Askov.

I did not want to move, but I had a different reason. I could not bear to leave the beautiful church in Askov. Our cozy little house on the prairie which Papa had built with his own hands was snug from the winter storms. I had my own secret hiding place in the woods where I went by myself to think about God and watch the yellow and black meadowlarks and the scarlet cardinals build their nests and raise their babies.

I've always longed to stay put. Years later as a pastor's wife, I would weep on every church step as the moving van left with our possessions. I remember once we moved after the church had just

built a new parsonage. I had never lived in a new
house and I had dreamed and planned every de-
tail of how I would decorate it. But we were called
to serve another church. I didn't want to do it. As
I sat defiantly on the church steps waiting for the
moving van, my husband put his arms around me,
lovingly sheltering me from my pain. "Aren't you
glad we are leaving this place better than we found
it?" he asked gently. And then I remembered that
moving day many years before when we left Askov
and God taught me that he always prepares the
way before us.

Papa took me to town for the last time and let
me say good-bye to the Askov church. He reminded
me there would be no rocks or stumps in Wisconsin. When I got home I found a matchbox and filled
it with rocks. I would be a celebrity—the only person in Wisconsin who had rocks—and I would
share them with all the children who had never
seen one. I would soon learn, however, that every
place we visit on life's pilgrimage has its share of
rocks.

The Roaring Twenties had left everyone unpre-
pared for the Great Depression. In Wisconsin Papa
could grow corn, but the bottom fell out of both
corn and hog prices. The banks closed and the
Roosevelt administration, even with its National
Recovery Act and New Deal, could not stop the
avalanche of foreclosures. The American Commu-
nist Party took to the streets demanding food.

Hitler was growing more powerful while broad-
casting his anti-Semitic gospel He promised to an-
nihilate the Jews and create a pure Aryan race.

Churches in Europe were empty. God's people were silent! Hitler was the savior who would destroy the church and fill the vacuum by solving every economic problem.

"Perhaps America needs a savior like Hitler," folks were saying. Papa was stunned. He violently disagreed.

Prices dropped out of farmland. Papa's 200 acres, which he bought for $10,000, were almost worthless. We all worked to survive. I was up early every morning, going to the barn to milk six cows before walking the two miles to our country school.

If a machine part broke, nobody could afford a new one. Instead, a person hunted for a bolt or barbed wire to fix it. I was so proud of Papa because it seemed there was no machine in the world he could not fix with just barbed wire.

But more than the depression was attacking our family. It had been twenty years since two wide-eyed, dream-filled Danish immigrants had been divided by class on the ocean steamer which brought them to the land of golden opportunity. Too many children born too close together, stumps and stones, the depression, the threat of foreclosure, grasshoppers, and prairie fires may have erased class distinctions. But it could not erase memories.

Perhaps in bitter moments of poverty and broken dreams, Holger remembered Rosa in her plush Danish *herre gård* and Mama remembered that her family was distantly related to royalty. In those times, it seemed that some of our family were drawn to Mama and some to Papa—and we became divided from each other. It was the same kind of division that had divided Mama's family. To me we seemed like little children at play who had to choose sides in a game none of us could possibly win. It seemed some were first class and some were fourth class, depending who you sided with.

I dearly loved Mama and often when I lay awake at night and the house was quiet and the moon shone daylight bright across the snowy stillness and the wind moaned through the winter willows, I wondered if Mama were awake, too, thinking of the great King's Church, the magnificent manor house where she had lived and the young men who had come courting. Then I would drift off to sleep dreaming of a Mama whose dreams had all come true. She was young and beautiful and rich and famous and all the things I knew Mama could have been and Papa was not able to help her become. Yes, I loved Papa, but I loved Mama, too, and I wished with all my heart that life could have been easier for her.

Papa sat at the peace table and said, "Nobody has to choose sides in a family." During long winter nights, after the chores were done and the kerosene lamp was lit, he would cut one apple in seven pieces, one for each of us. He would gather us all together around the long homemade table and read wonderful Danish books out loud, *Gønge Høvdingen* and *Peer Gynt*.

I didn't know anything about first or fourth class. I only knew that my one source of strength was Papa and the church. God had provided another beautiful church for us in Wisconsin. Huddled in the back of our wagon, a homemade comforter shielding us from the hay, we jostled the long miles to the West Denmark Lutheran Church. As we neared the church Mama would check our faces and hands and give us a spit bath where needed. As we entered the church doors, we were ushered to a front pew. An enormous hand-carved altar with Thorvaldson's wonderful marble statue of Jesus reached its outstretched arms toward us and gazed at us with loving, compassionate eyes. Painted in the background were angels wearing long white trailing monk's robes tied with a heavy cord. To my amazement, this Wisconsin church had exactly the same wooden altar as the church in Askov, expertly carved by the same Danish wood-carver, Jes Schmidt. God was indeed somewhere, if only I could find him.

Our pastor, Rev. Koch, wearing a honeycombed clerical collar and long black robe, preached from a pulpit elevated high on the wall. Each Sunday as I sat beside Papa, I felt secure and warm. I was certain that if I got to heaven, God would look exactly like Rev. Koch—tall, dark, and handsome with a warm and winning smile. His beautiful, stately wife, Dora, played Bach, Schumann, and the Danish hymns on the lovely old organ. As I sat there each Sunday with Papa's big hand engulfing mine, it seemed for a moment that life was sweeter and dearer than I could ever imagine.

In a harsh and bitter world, the church was the one anchor for all the storms of life. I had fallen hopelessly and incurably in love with it, although

I did not understand the church at all. I did not
understand God. But in a world of depression and
misunderstandings, poverty and pain, for one
whole hour each week something was different.
When we were there it was the answer to all I
would ever need in life. Was it there on the
heartstrings of my life so long ago that I first heard
the sound of heaven I could never escape? As the
psalmist David wrote, "As the deer pants for
streams of water, so my soul pants for you, O God"
(Psalm 42:1).

Sitting on the shiny, hand-hewn pew, wedged
between two troubled parents, I sensed that inside
the walls of this building, elusive as it was, lay an
answer to all I would ever need in life. But how
to find it for myself and for my father?—that was
the quest, the impossible dream.

The amazing and miraculous joy was that my
father bonded with Rev. Koch. Papa understood
my need to find God and made a very special point
of helping the pastor get to know me. Whenever
possible, Papa would find time to talk with him,
always letting me tag along. Before we left, Rev.
Koch would always touch my head or put his hand
on my shoulder. Nothing gave me more self-esteem. Today pastors are afraid to touch people, but
since we are ninety-nine percent skin, the need is
still there. That simple touch from a man of God
gave me courage for another week.

Once a month folks stayed after church for
selskab (fellowship dinner). Somehow poverty and
hard times would fade for one afternoon. The men
would set up sawhorses and wooden planks which

the ladies covered with bed sheets for tablecloths. Like manna from above, God sent homemade cakes and breads, Danish *rullepølse, kødboller* (meat balls) and *æblekage* (Danish apple cake). As I savored food so exquisitely delightful compared to our harsh everyday fare, I would think I was in heaven. God seemed to be in charge and had not forgotten about us. As the delicious aroma filled the air and it came my turn to fill my plate, I felt secure. Yes, God had his eye on us.

If someone had recently visited Denmark, immigrants hungry for news of the homeland listened to lengthy speeches and asked endless questions. In summer while the speeches droned on, the children donned homemade swim suits and dived into nearby Butternut Lake.

In the winter folks tuned up their fiddles. They began with the grand old hymns from the Psalter of the Danish hymn book. Soon those lonely pioneer immigrants pushed back the tables and sang nostalgically of Danebrog and Denmark as if there were no ocean between America and their homeland and no depression outside.

While the fiddles sang and the clapping and toe tapping lasted, Rev. Koch enveloped his people in a blanket of warmth and love. For those few hours we could almost believe what the president had promised—that prosperity was just around the corner and soon there would be a chicken in every pot and a car in every garage.

The highlight of the summer was the Danish Summer School. Here for three months the children of Danish immigrants were taught to read and write Danish, to learn the old Grundtvig hymns, the folk tunes, folk dances and stories of the old country. Here in a strange land across the sea, immigrant parents could imbue their children with the richness of the heritage of their fatherland. Here children lived for an entire summer in the loving atmosphere created by Rev. Koch.

How I longed to go to Danish Summer School. But we lived too far away, and we had no money. So I looked with envy at those who lived closer, whose parents found a way to send them in spite of everything. My brothers and sisters laughed at me, thinking it sheer foolishness to want to go to school in summer.

But all of God's lessons that summer were not in Danish. He taught me that when you aren't able to set the sails on the winds of adversity, God will provide a hiding place, a shelter in the time of storm. He always is waiting to use our disasters to shape our destiny.

Through many years of ministry, God was to prove that over and over in my life. Each time God sent my husband to a new church, it always had exactly the things our family needed: a loving first-grade teacher, an accomplished pianist who offered free lessons, a college where my husband could earn graduate credits while pastoring the church, a grandmother who adopted our children. Or, if these were absent, we received lessons in patience and reliance that would last a lifetime.

Now I see that God was preparing me throughout my childhood so that when he sent me to work with troubled children, or with pastors or their wives, I could teach that precious truth with authenticity.

Miracles have always come stealing into my life as if on the soft pillowed feet of a kitten, just when I least expect them. Rev. Koch sensed my deep spiritual hunger and my father sensed my yearning for the church and God. On a balmy May Sunday morning after the pastor had announced summer school and I could hardly stand the idea that I could not go, Mrs. Koch sought me out after church.

"The garden is so big, and I have so little time to weed it," she began almost apologetically, "and your Papa tells me how good you are at that. I need help with my children, too, when I'm busy doing things for church. I just don't see how I can manage without some help. Would you like to stay with us and give me a hand so I can have more time to work for God? I can't pay you, but you could go to Danish summer school."

Her words were like sun shining in the middle of a rain storm. Birds were singing somewhere in my heart and there was not a cloud in the sky. God had to be around. Even though I hadn't found him and he didn't owe me any miracles, he had come through!

Looking back, I now realize how little Mrs. Koch needed another mouth to feed. A gallon of milk cost 5 cents, a sack of flour was 29 cents, a slab of bacon 35 cents, but who had 35 cents? Nevertheless, the way she worded her invitation made me feel nine feet tall. She said she needed me. To think that someone really needed me! What music! What joy! Charity is only charity if it doesn't cost you your self-esteem.

The next Sunday Papa left me and a paper sack containing my extra dress at the parsonage after church. Mama thought it was *nar* foolishness. Papa held me tight and said, "God has opened a door for you. Make sure you use it with care and enter it with gratitude."

During the long days I had been bedfast after being scalded, I had hungered to read. We had few English books but we did have a Sears Roebuck catalog filled with stylish ladies wearing lavish gowns, men in fancy coats, and children dressed like royalty. There were hundreds of pictures of mysterious washing machines you didn't have to work to make go, heating stoves, curtains, and cars. Best of all, each picture had words to match the pictures. During that long winter of pain, my five-year-old mind was busy learning to read. I asked Mama and Papa endless questions. It seemed such play and it opened a whole new world of reading to me.

Now at age seven I was learning to read Danish. Much more glorious than that, I was living in the shadow of the church steeple and under the same roof as God's wonderful servants, the Kochs. It was an ambivalent, strange feeling. Though I dearly missed Papa, for the first time in my life I felt wanted, as though I belonged and was really at home. Each morning I woke to hear Mrs. Koch practising Bach or the great hymns of the church. Through a half-closed door I often saw Rev. Koch on his knees, the morning sunlight streaming through the window. Often I could slip into the sanctuary and sit quietly drinking in beauty so serene and sacred music so heavenly I would weep for joy. My love affair with the church was born long before I knew who God was. "Before they call I will answer" (Isaiah 65:24).

Today churches all over America are dying. Throughout my life, my call has been to revive dying churches around the world. Nobody should grow up so poor they do not have a church all their own. From that day to this, it seems unbelievable to me that just when America stands at the crossroads—when children need hopes and dreams more than ever—we let the church die!

It is the calamity of the century for which America will pay dearly! No government agency, no social program can ever replace the vital, loving, soul-winning church. Unless we learn from history we are bound to repeat it. I always view the decline or death of a church as the greatest tragedy on earth. I know how the church can shape for a lifetime—for better or for worse—every soul who passes by.

I think Papa sensed the noble thing Mrs. Koch had done in inviting me to live with them that summer—a seven-year-old, after all, might prove to be more trouble than help—but he did not object. Papa was grateful I could go to Danish Summer School, but he was not about to accept charity.

On the Monday night of this arrangement, just as the sun was blazing on the horizon, God sent his next miracle. I couldn't believe it. Coming down the dirt road was Papa with his hay wagon loaded with old Bess, my favorite milk cow, as a gift for the preacher. "I just noticed your pasture behind the church," Papa explained to Mrs. Koch as he stood at the parsonage door. "My pasture is mighty poor this year and I just thought you might be able to give my cow some feed this summer. Rose can milk the cow, so it shouldn't be any bother to have old Bess around."

Danes are proud people and they don't accept charity easily. I quickly figured out the game Mrs. Koch and Papa were playing. My joy was unspeakable as I realized Papa had thought me worth a whole milk cow! I also learned a lesson I never forgot. Even when we don't dare ask for miracles, God often heaps them on us anyway.

Papa knew that Bess would bring dignity for me and a sense of worth that I needed so much. I would not feel entirely like a charity case and I would have an old familiar friend in the back pasture. Since Papa had taught me how to milk, every morning and night I felt a closeness to him as I milked old Bess and brought in the foaming pail of good warm milk for the parsonage table. God's angels supplied all our needs—dignity for me and milk for the preacher's young family.

The Kochs were two people deeply in love, purpose-driven by their love for each other and the community. I remember Rev. Koch saying from the pulpit again and again: "God has something special for those who save something special for someone special." I determined that one day I would have that kind of marriage. I would never marry,

I decided, until I could find a preacher who looked and lived exactly like Rev. Koch because I was certain he looked and lived exactly like God.

That resolve was sorely tested during high school when I had no home and worked as a maid in a home with five twenty-something men in the household, all with gutter morals. I knew I dared not offer my life to God tarnished. I thank God I had learned about guardian angels. They were indeed real and enormously necessary.

God was directing my destiny during those days I spent in the Kochs' home. One night while I was deep into my homework I looked up and was amazed to see Rev. Koch gazing at me intently. "Rose, I know you would make a great teacher," he said. I was shocked. I had never thought I was good enough to be a teacher. Except for Papa's love, I had often felt unwanted, ugly, and of little worth. I lisped and could not say my R's and my clothes were faded, too short or too long and handed down twice before they came to me. I had bright red hair and my sunburned complexion curdled into huge brown freckles.

Eternity was in that moment. That day my goals were set. If that wonderful man of God thought I would make a great teacher, I knew I could and would be a teacher.

Many years later I taught in an inner city school. One of my students was a tiny, poverty-stricken ragamuffin from a family of thirteen children with no father. One morning she came to school very excited and could scarcely wait to tell me, "Teacher, I saw you down town with dat man."

"Honey, that man was my husband."

"You lives with him all de time?" Alisha retorted.

"For twenty-five years."

"Shore must get powerful boresome," was her astonished reply. She had never seen a family that was committed not just for better or worse, but for good.

Later, as I was busily helping students at their desks I looked up and saw little Alisha sitting behind my large desk with her pencil behind her ear, just where I always tucked mine so that my hands would be free to hug or help a student. I could see she was dreaming of being me—a real teacher, a somebody, not just an unwanted welfare waif.

With memories flooding my soul, and a prayer in my heart, I went to her, kneeling down to minimize the difference in our sizes. I encircled her in my arms and paid back the favor I had received many long years before.

"Alisha," I said to her, "I know you would make a great teacher." I kept that dream alive in her heart as long as I was in that school. When I returned years later I was thrilled to see her teaching in that same school.

We all owe so many debts we must remember to repay.

Chapter Seven

Dying Grace

*D*uring those next years, I spent every summer with the Kochs and much of the winters. During those formative years, time and again I found solitude and peace by slipping quietly over to the church next door to sit there held close by those hallowed walls. I fantacized that I would grow up to marry a minister. He would look exactly like Rev. Koch and one day I would play the great organ. My children would sit in the pew, rich in their nearness to God because their father was the pastor and they lived in God's house.

Mrs. Koch buried deep in my heart a love of good music. I believe a nation rises and falls on its music and unfortunately it seems we have taken the melody out of music. She taught me the basic notes and let me play on her little pump

organ in the parsonage. Soon I was picking out
tunes and filling in with the harmony. But I
wanted to learn more. My older sister, Ruth,
sensed this hunger. When a neighbor offered to
give her music lessons in return for doing house-
work, she asked if she could also get music lessons
for me.

When Mama sent Papa to an auction to bid on
a washing machine and there was none for sale,
he bid his only dollar on an ornate organ. In the
depth of the depression he had no competition and
came home with the eight-foot intricately carved
pump organ. I shall always be grateful. I would
need this knowledge badly in ministry and was
able to pass that gift on to my children and they
to theirs.

Everyone's life is a fairy tale written by God.
My very best friend and only confidant in the Danish community was Helga. Her large immigrant
family lived up the lane from the church. We read
our Danish lessons together, memorized our catechism, and made castles for the woodland fairies
down in the glen where we had our secret hiding
place.

We often talked about how we could find God.
No question about God was off limits: Who made
God? Was he married? Where did Cain get a wife?
Again and again, almost as if she had a premoni-
tion of death, Helga would ask, "Can anyone really and truly know for sure where they go when
they die?"

These were questions Papa and I had dis-
cussed, but never concluded. Some of them seemed

too foolish to ask Pastor Koch, some just too personal.

Early Danish pioneers, far from their fatherland, brought old-world customs to America. The church was an exact replica of the village churches in Denmark. On Sunday mornings the bell pealed melodically, "Ding Dong, Come to Church," and I felt close to God. But when the bell tolled for a death I panicked, especially when the church bell dolefully pealed out in the middle of the silent night, or in a thunderstorm, or during a blizzard. It was eery and awesome as it rang the years— one at a time—of the departed one's life span.

Death was so frightening. Many people in our community had died, some of smallpox, some of polio or whooping cough. You only live once, but you are dead such a long, long time. Where was everyone who had died? Was God angry with me because I was not always good? Would I be afraid when my time came to die? I cautiously asked Rev. Koch a few of my questions.

"Don't worry," he told me. "When you die, God will give you dying grace. Why should he give it to you now and have you carry it around for eighty-some years?"

That made sense, and I put death out of my mind, at least until the next time the bell rang . . . this time forty times. Holger Hansen had been out in a boat with his children and the Kochs' children when he had a heart attack and fell out of the boat. Hearing the children scream, Rev. Koch dived into the water and swam out to the boat. He barely saved the children, but could not save Mr. Hansen.

I quickly subtracted my nine years and consoled myself that even thirty-one years is a long time. I wondered, where was Mr. Hansen now? Did he have dying grace? How did he get it? My questions were so personal I even hesitated to ask Papa. And yet I wondered: Was death the final sleep or the final awakening?

Late one stifling summer day the sky hung in an eerie yellow stillness, breathlessly awaiting a tornado. I was in the field bringing Bess home when I heard the church bell ring seven, *pause,* eight, *pause,* nine, *pause* . . . and no more!

I stood mesmerized, oblivious to the rain clouds and lightning that were filling the sky. Was someone playing with the church bell? No, there had been a solid five seconds between each ring. I saw the sun sink unwillingly beneath a murky, foreboding sky. Was God's sun setting on someone's life?

"Ring again," I whispered out loud. "God, make that bell ring again. Nine-year-olds DO NOT die."

Thunder rolled, pounding its way across the darkening meadow. Rain was pelting the earth. Lightning was flashing. However, a far greater storm was brewing in my soul. Death, which I had pushed out of my mind and heart—the God Papa and I had talked about but never found—was talking! Loudly and clearly! I stood alone in the solitude of that storm, alone in the dark black meadow of my pilgrimage to find God. I was afraid to go! I was afraid to stay! I did not know God! I had never found him. Maybe it was too late. So many had died. Maybe I would be next.

Finally, after what seemed like an eternity, the roaring wind began to reluctantly abate. The sun had long since gone to rest. I had not even noticed that Bess had already found her way back into the shelter of the barn. Rain, cold and dismal, was soaking me to the very bone. A nine-year-old had died! Whom did I know who was nine?

What a wonderful compassionate God we have! In the middle of that storm, just like the disciples on the sea, I learned that God comes walking toward us through the storms. I stumbled and fell as I slogged across the waterlogged coal-black stubble and . . . there at the gate stood Papa.

Word spreads fast in closely knit communities. As soon as he heard that my friend had drowned in the farm pond where we often swam, Papa had hooked up the wagon and hurried to find me. He held me close.

"It was Helga," Papa said softly.

I pounded his chest. I cried out to God: "God, if you are there, tell me why!" I wanted to hear the voice of God roaring an excuse from heaven. But all I heard was the lightning crashing and the thunder roaring.

I think I grew up that day.

When I could finally utter the words, I said to Papa, "There has to be an answer." The special bond between us deepened that day.

When I could weep no more and lay limp in his arms, Papa said, "Yes, nine-year-olds can die." He didn't have to ask what I was thinking. Papa knew.

"But, Papa, where did she go?"

Circled in Papa's big strong arms, I thought he would explain to me exactly why a good God would take the only real childhood companion I had ever had. And why Helga? Good, kind, laughing Helga, whose long blonde pigtails always danced in the sunlight as we ran across the meadow. SHE HAD DIED! Surely God did not need her as much as I needed a best friend. God had so many and I had just Helga and Papa. But good, strong Papa, who could fix anything and knew everything, could not fix Helga and he did not know for sure where she was.

I knew that I did not know where Helga had gone when she died. I also knew that Papa and I did not know where *we* would go if we died. I remembered how often she had talked about death. Why hadn't I found out before she died so I could have told her? I lived with the preacher's family. Helga's family did not go to church. I should have known the answer. I was to blame. If only I had known how Helga could get ready for heaven, I would have left no stone unturned to make sure she knew before God took her away.

Had she been able to find the God I had not been able to find as we held our song books together at catechism and sang *"Dejlig er Jorden, Prægtig er Guds Himmel* (Beautiful Savior, Beautiful Heaven)"?

I sat numbly between Papa and Mama as they buried Helga. Mrs. Koch played the great organ. The music swelled to the steeple while I sat there angry and afraid of God. I was angry at life and too afraid of my thoughts about God and death to ask Rev. Koch. They sang about God and heaven. I didn't understand the God they were singing about. Helga's Mama stood up and testified that God needed Helga. That made no sense. Heaven must have plenty of children without taking Helga. I decided I would wait for just the right time and then I would ask Rev. Koch how anyone could know for certain they had a home in heaven and why in the world God needed Helga just now when we were having so much fun and had so many plans for living.

I wanted to see Helga again . . . if she were in heaven. If not, then where? I had heard a visiting preacher talk about hell. Who made hell? Surely Helga could not be there. If so, since I let Helga go there, I didn't stand a chance. I shuddered. I knew there must be an answer. But if the church couldn't tell us, then why did we have a church at all?

Years later when I headed a university's Psychology department, each semester I would ask my students to take out a sheet of paper.

"This is not a test," I would instruct. "Just write what you think about most, but never talk about."

At least ninety-five percent of the time, the paper would have one large, bold word: "DEATH."

Chapter Eight

Papa's Love Skis

Yes, I would ask Rev. Koch my questions about death at the right time. But the right time never came. Another storm was brewing.

The young people who gathered at the parish house each Saturday night for dancing and fiddle playing wanted to invite their American friends to worship. They wanted services in English.

"Vat foolishness. Danish is no longer gut enuf?" some people said.

The old folks argued that no scripture is half as melodic in English as in Danish. I can understand how they felt. To this day I sometimes weep at the beauty of the Lord's prayer in Danish, "*Fadervor, du som er i himmel* (Our Father, who art in heaven)," and the great Danish hymns such as "*Alt stor i Gud Fader's hånd, Hvad han vil, det ved hans ånd* (Life is in the Father's hand, What he wills, is his command)."

West Denmark, like Askov, had built its church as an exact replica of the lovely country churches in Denmark. People wanted their churches to remain exactly like the churches where they had grown up.

The bureaucracy of the church was not helping. The denomination was filled with strife about the confession ordinants had to sign. A new group forming within the Lutheran church, called the Inner Mission Society, felt the church was too liberal. They opposed dancing, shows, and many other newfangled ideas the church refused to condemn.

The great depression was on. Tempers were short.

"I may have given up my Fatherland, but I'll be switched if I'll give up my beloved mother tongue," someone said at a meeting that was called one hot summer day before our monthly potluck.

"Ya, ya," another shouted. "Nobody will ever take da Danish from our church . . . not while I'm alive."

A pioneer who had led the building of the church stood up to shout, "Da bank has already taken my farm, pneumonia has taken my wife, and now da preacher wants to take over the church WE built. Maybe it's time to get another preacher."

Rev. Koch was caught squarely in the middle. I listened as he pleaded and offered compromises. He said he could preach two Sundays in Danish and two in English, or perhaps an early service in

English and the 11 o'clock service in Danish. Others began complaining about the dancing.

"The recreation on Saturday night is not in the sanctuary," he explained, "but in the parish house—totally separate from the church building. The depression has left a great vacuum both socially and spiritually. If the church does not fill it for the young people, the devil will."

It seemed to me Rev. Koch was wasting his breath.

Then Papa stood up. Because he seldom spoke out, you could have heard a pin drop in the parish hall basement.

"I've been thinking," he began softly, "that God isn't going to hold us responsible for saving the whole world, or our farms, or even this denomination. He is going to hold us totally accountable for our little corner here at West Denmark. If our church dies, it won't be the depression or the devil closing it—it will be us!

"Look, the church is packed with young people and kids on Saturday night and Sunday morning. They even hang around the church all week long. If they were not spending time here, where do you think they would be? Soon these kids will be running our world. They can live without our farms, but can they do without our faith?

"Ja, Lars," Papa continued, addressing the pioneer who had spoken, "by the time this is all over none of us may have a farm to give our children for an inheritance. But if we kill our church, they will lose much more than a farm. They will lose their faith! That's the inheritance they need most."

Then Papa sat down. I stared at him in amazement. Had he found God or had his futile search simply made him more determined to save the church so he would have somewhere to keep looking?

Mrs. Koch went to the piano and softly started playing *Du Store Gud.* I could smell the coffee in the church kitchen. I was surprised to see that in the dimness of the parish hall basement Papa seemed to have grown ten feel tall.

But by now the church was split. Folks were taking sides. Papa's speech may have helped for a while, but too much had been said that could not be unsaid. Pretty soon it seemed to have nothing to do with anything in the church. "They aren't even talking about God any more. It is just a power struggle," Papa said to Mama one day. "It is just pure *nar* foolishness!"

Papa told me that people who spend their lives fighting their churches or families or marriages never have time for greatness. The struggle consumes all their lives. He said it is best to move quietly away from troubles that you see no hope of solving and go on to do something noble that could change the world for the better.

Maybe he was remembering Mama's family in Denmark. He mentioned Uncle Emil, Mama's youngest brother, who was a brilliant agronomist. He had escaped the turmoil in their family by quietly moving to Ho Laido, Japan, with his wife and children. There he worked as a representative of the Danish government seeking to bring healing between the two nations before World War II.

The Japanese people were hungry. But they were also very proud and unwilling to accept help from outsiders. Uncle Emil, in great wisdom, bought a barren mountain side that was unfit for agriculture. He cut down trees, fenced the land, planted the barren soil in clover, and turned out cows to pasture. As they ate the grass, they also devoured every new shoot of brush seeking to reclaim the land. Soon his cows were giving five times the milk of other cows in the region. When the land was thoroughly cleared, Uncle Emil planted dozens of varieties of fruits and vegetables never before grown in Japan.

He did not preach. He waited for the harvest and then lovingly took his produce to market. He packaged seeds and seedlings and hired a few Japanese people to help him, knowing they would go home to teach others how to clear land, increase milk production, and market these marvelous new fruits and vegetables. Those Japanese teachers became heroes. In the end, few remembered who first brought the wonderful fruits to Japan. But hunger was averted for many a desperate Japanese family as their country weathered a crisis.

All his life Uncle Emil longed for his fatherland. Turmoil pains even the innocent. Finally his work was done. His children were spread around the world. His son had engineered the building of the subway systems in Honolulu, San Francisco, and Atlanta. His daughters were leaders in education.

Unkel Emil and *Tante* Fritz went home to Denmark to die. They bought a tiny cottage by the sea and grew strawberries as big as teacups. Their little villa boasted succulent pears and peaches. They went to church where they sang again in the familiar tongue the hymns they had sung for a lifetime in a faraway land.

Yes, turmoil had exacted its price. But on the wall of that humble cottage hung the highest award the Emperor of Japan had ever given a foreigner for meritorious service.

Papa told me, "Remember that when someone tells you they hold all the cards, they are only playing solitaire. Causing trouble consumes all of your life and keeps you from greatness. Solve problems if you can but if you can't, move away from them."

It was advice I was to remember all my life. Long after I was grown I could remembered Papa telling me, "All of God's children are called to greatness. No one can keep you from greatness without your permission." He often quoted the serenity prayer: "God grant me the courage to change the things I can change, to accept what I can't change, and the wisdom to know the difference."

Throughout that summer church members argued, "Ja, da children must learn de Danish. How vil day learn it if vi cannot read *Gud's Ord* (God's Holy Word) in Danish? Vi vil not read da Holy Bible in dat funny language." But their language of conflict seemed to me to be quite unholy and not a bit funny.

Perhaps church life would have been simpler if times had been prosperous. But times were hard. While President Hoover preached that "prosperity was just around the corner," 85 percent of Toledo was unemployed. The government licensed 6,500 apple vendors and pencil sellers. The wolf was at the door. America was on the road to rock bottom. Some 100,000 auto workers were laid off in just the city of Detroit. One fourth of the banks were closed and the Red Cross ran out of aid.

Farmers experienced nationwide drought. The Midwest was a veritable dust bowl. Oakies seeking jobs in California died of hunger, heat, and thirst in the railway cars they jumped to travel to that mecca. For months on end there was no rain. Every day in June and July it seemed that the temperature rose over a hundred degrees. Corn dried up before it was inches high. The government distributed garden seeds—pumpkins, collards, corn—but who could get them to grow with no rain?

President Hoover kept saying welfare was not necessary if only people would work. Mama was at her wit's end. Papa worked. He never walked. He ran. He was up before the sun and worked until long after it retired. There was no corn to cultivate, and what there was brought only seven cents a bushel. Folks were burning it for fuel to keep warm. The cows were drying up and dropping their calves. Papa searched for odd jobs.

Yet I never knew we were poor. I had Papa and we built memories.

That winter I wanted more than anything to have a real lunch bucket to replace the syrup pail. It would be especially glorious if it had a thermos. How comforting it would be to walk the two miles to school carrying a real store-bought lunch bucket, its magical thermos defying the freezing winter with piping hot soup hidden inside. I fantasized about how it would save me if I were someday stranded in a blizzard.

I looked for the lunch bucket under the Christmas tree every year. It never came, but one year God substituted something even more wonderful.

That year none of us had dared ask for anything for Christmas. There was no money for the mortgage. Farms all around us had been sold at auction. The neighbors had banded together to save a few farms from foreclosure by bidding one cent on a tractor and one cent on a farm and then boycotting all other bids until the bank was forced to accept that one ridiculous bid and return the farm to its original—and very astonished—owner.

Such miracles stood out clearly in my mind. I reasoned that if there were a God and if he could perform an enormous miracle such as saving a whole farm, maybe I should test him by asking him to provide skis to transport us the two long miles to our country school during the subzero Wisconsin winters. If he could produce the skis, then I could believe that he would somehow save Papa's farm.

The dream for those skis began in the outhouse. In a big family, privacy is of the essence. When I lived with the Kochs I could go next door to the church, but at home I found my solitude in the outhouse.

It was a wonderful place because it housed the Montgomery Ward catalog, which was filled with dreams enough to last a lifetime. For a brief moment I could be the grand ladies in their store-bought finery or the rich children with porcelain dolls with painted pink faces and long golden curls tied up in real satin ribbons.

God also used that catalog to teach me how foolish the world's value system could be. One day I found a picture of a rabbit skin cape. I took the catalog into the house and showed it to my sister. We laughed at those capes on sale for $29.95. Our brother shot dozens of rabbits—big fat ones—all the time with his twenty-two rifle. He skinned them and we fried them crisp and brown and served them swimming in rich gravy, accompanied by potatoes and home-canned beans. Why, we hardly kept the rabbit skins. We sold them for a nickel if we could find someone dumb enough to buy them. "The kids at school would laugh their heads off if we came to school in plain ole' rabbit skins," said my sister. "Nobody in their right mind would spend hard-earned money for such nonsense."

The catalog did contain thousands of real treasures, however. Snow skis, for one thing. Now they made sense! With them you could get to school faster and be out of the biting cold in half the time.

Since my older sister Ruth worked with Papa in the fields it was decided she would hint to him about the skis. He talked to me about them but gave me little hope.

I wasn't as keen on the skis as I was on seeing a whopper of a miracle. I needed to know if God could really pull one off for us.

When Christmas came and we sang the old Danish carols, I noticed right away that there was nothing that looked even remotely like skis under our Christmas tree.

We had all gone to the woods to help Papa cut the fragrant ceiling-high fir. Earlier on *Juleaften* (Christmas Eve) we had decorated it with popcorn, cranberries, and Danish flags. Then we had closed it away in the parlor until after our wonderful Christmas supper of roast pork, red cabbage, and *æblekage* (Danish apple cake) with thick sweet whipped cream.

After the feast, Papa and Mama slipped away to light the tiny wax candles in their marvelous little brass holders that decorated our Christmas tree. Then they opened the parlor doors. In wide-eyed splendor we entered a magical world where there was no poverty, no depression, no unhappy families—nothing but an angel on the very top of the tree and tiny candles glowing in the mystical night as everyone sang *Glædelig Jule* (Silent Night) in the nostalgic Danish tongue of our immigrant parents.

There was an orange for everyone. We made them last as long as we could, eating every bit smack down to the last bitter bite of golden rind. And there was a wonderful sack of hard candy. It was the one we had gotten at the school program but Papa made us save it for this night because there was no money for candy. I marveled at the tiny baby Jesus and the manger etched in the red, gold, and green hard candy. We thought it almost sacrilegious to eat it but succumbed to the delectable minty sweetness. My brothers would eat all their candy right away but I would save mine, eating one piece a week, making it last almost until summer.

Then the miracle I shall never forget happened. There was the jingle of Claire, Hans, and Daisy's sleighbells on the roof. Then a raucous man just Papa's height and build wearing a Santa mask came ho-ho-ing through the door carrying not just one pair of skis, but a homemade—Papa-made—pair for each of us.

The next day after the cows were milked, we tucked our long-legged underwear into our black woolen home-knit socks, put on our four-buckle overshoes, mittens, scarves, and hand-me-down coats, and began the task of learning to ski. By the time we returned to school after Christmas we could handle those skis.

The opulent splendor of speeding across the long-since-harvested wheat field on brand new skis, defying the six-foot snowbanks piled high against the fence rows, made me forget all about my dream of a store-bought lunch bucket. I was on my way to show my classmates the new skis Papa had meticulously made for me out of two mere pieces of pine board carved to a fine point, painstakingly sanded and then submerged under pressure in boiling water to curve at just the right angle. A piece of leather salvaged from Daisy's old harness provided the straps. Oh, they were super skis.

When we arrived at school we held our heads high with a new prestige. Most kids had gotten

nothing for Christmas but Papa had figured out
how to get us out of the cold in half the time and
with twice the fun. I boasted with an amazing lack
of humility that my Papa could do anything!

Chapter Nine

Where Are You, God? I Need You!

*T*he farm was not miraculously saved, but something far more valuable was salvaged from those depression years of my childhood. I learned the fortitude Papa showed during those dark days when he did lose the farm. It was the same kind of grit he had demonstrated through crop failures, drought, cyclones, Russian thistles, and grasshoppers. It was exactly the stuff I would later need to help me answer my call to missions.

One fall God taught me another necessary lesson. Thirty children attended our one-room schoolhouse. I was the only girl so I thought I had privileged status. I was appointed to clean the school every night after school, for which I received a whole dollar a month. Our teacher, Miss Marcott, was paid $25 a month. She boarded with a family and out of that salary paid her "keep" and the one-dollar janitor's salary. She came early in the morning and had to have the school warm by the time we arrived. At night she dared not send any of us home until we were carefully bundled with nothing but our eyes showing between the scarves and overcoats.

Since I was the only girl and could play the piano, and since the school Halloween and Christmas programs were the big social events of the year, I was the star. I was the mother, the teacher, the angel, the piano player in every play. For once I felt really needed. In fact, for the first time in my life I felt quite indispensable. They just couldn't have programs without me, I reasoned.

After school on the night of our big Halloween program I was sweeping up. Everyone had gone home but the teacher and me. That's when I decided to test my strength. I told Miss Marcott that I felt very sick and probably would not take part in the program that night. Now, in reality wild horses could not have kept me away, but the teacher was worried. She was an excellent teacher but it seemed her job depended more on good Halloween and Christmas programs than on her teaching abilities.

I rushed home, milked my cows, and was back at school with bells on in time to be the star of the Halloween show. I didn't even remember that I had lied to the teacher.

The next morning as I milked my cows the applause of the previous night rang in my ears. All the way to school I fantasized about being the shining star of our next performance, the Christmas play. After that triumph, all the students would forget that I lisped, that my dress was faded and handed-down, that I was a fourth-class outsider only Papa could love.

I arrived at school eager for more adulation, but Miss Marcott offered nothing but a stony, "Good morning."

Even before the bell rang and we found our seats I sensed that something was wrong. The clock ticked noisily on the wall. The teacher's Comfort shoes squeaked as she came from behind her desk to solemnly announce, "Today I am passing out the parts for the Christmas program."

My heart was pounding. The Christmas program was the climax of the entire year. It was the season of joy, the time to shine. Why did the teacher look so deadly serious?

Already I saw myself as Mary, the mother of God. I would wear white sheets and look angelic. The cherubs would all sing for me. Everyone would be mad at the innkeeper for turning me away. Besides the nativity pageant we always presented a "soap box opera" play and I would play the patient mother, the pathetic heroine, or the lonely little match girl. After all, I was now a seasoned actress, indispensable and famous.

"Gerald, will you please stand up," intoned Miss Marcott.

He stood slowly, unsure of what would happen next.

"Yes, you will do quite well for Mary. You will have to keep your back to the audience and wear a shawl. That way everyone can concentrate on seeing the most important person, the baby Jesus," Miss Marcott told the stunned boy.

My heart was pounding. If Gerry would be Mary, the mother of God, that must mean the teacher had an even bigger part for me!

"I have chosen an unusual play this year," Miss Marcott continued. "It is about a widowed father with six sons. Ole, you will be the father."

I had read her play books and knew the play she had chosen. Apparently Miss Marcott had killed off the mother and made the hero a widower.

One by one, she assigned parts to all the boys.

The piano, I thought. *She will have to use me for the piano. I am the only one who can play, even though I can only play with two fingers.*

Then from under her desk the teacher produced a small windup victrola and a big, fat victrola record that contained all the Christmas carols.

"We will sing with this," she announced.

I realized then that Miss Marcott knew my secret. I had not been sick. I had been healthy as a horse. I had just wanted to get attention, to be an insider. And I had wanted it badly enough to lie.

Surely everyone in the class would suspect that there was some reason I had been excluded from the Christmas program. What would Mama say? And dear, honest, kind Papa would be ashamed of me. All the parents would find out at the Christmas program; how could I face them? More than that, how could I face God? If God were really angry with me, how would I ever find him? Papa would never be able to keep his promise.

Silence descended on that tiny one-room school-house. The only sound was the drum beat of the large Seth Thomas clock as it pounded out eternity. Every eye, including God's, was directly on me.

Miss Marcott stood there in her one unadorned black dress that reached halfway down her calf, her horn-rimmed glasses perched on the end of her nose, her pointer in her hand. She was the judge and jury, and the verdict was in. I was guilty!

Finally, after the longest forever I had ever endured, Miss Marcott instructed us to take out our reading books.

But how could I think about reading when the sky was falling? How would I face the others at recess?

Miss Marcott took care of that. She asked me to stay inside during recess and sent all the others out. We talked long and hard and I learned lessons to last a lifetime.

Deeply remorseful, I begged for forgiveness and silently prayed she would change her mind about the punishment. She didn't. But after recess she did announce to the class: "We need someone to pull the curtains for the Christmas program, and I've asked Rose to do that." The curtains were bed sheets stretched across a wire.

I knew Miss Marcott was right. It was a painful lesson to learn. When we feel God can't do his work without our help, he can always relegate our talents to pulling curtains. I hope I never forget that lesson. God doesn't need us as much as we need him.

God was preparing me in other ways for mission work. For example, my school lunches were usually thick slices of homemade bread and jelly. Once in a great while it was peanut butter which Mama mixed with lard to make it go further. A rich and rather obese boy named Raymond attended our school. I knew he was rich because he rode a pony to school and was the only child in his family. Every single day he had chocolate marshmallow store-bought cookies in his store-bought lunch bucket and, on top of that, piping hot chocolate in his thermos.

I had never tasted one of those cookies but grudgingly watched him stuff them into his chubby little face two at a time. *What a waste of money,* I thought longingly. *If I had just one of those I'd make it last all week.*

At noon he would go out to feed his small horse. One day he asked me to go with him. As we stood there he devoured six of those cookies faster than a gnat could bat an eyelash. His chubby cheeks could hold no more. He held the last cookie out toward me as he told me how he hated them. It was the closest I had ever come to such a divine delicacy and my heart was racing faster than a jackrabbit with our old hound dog in pursuit. I was sure he was going to give it to me. I could already taste the rich dark brown chocolate. There was even enough to share. Then . . . he fed it to his horse!

I told that story during a children's sermon many years later. The next Sunday there was a whole box of those wonderful chocolate marshmallow cookies on the pulpit with my name on them. They didn't taste as good as that one would have way back then, but I knew I had taught the church that we have to be hungry with the hungry, lonely with the lonely, homeless with the homeless, forgotten with the forgotten. The way to soften one's own troubles is to remedy those of others.

As winter deepened gas companies turned off the heat. One woman asked if she could keep it on until she finished cooking supper, but the gas man turned it off. Then he noticed she was cooking her dog.

There were riots on the streets and bands of vigilantes were everywhere. Pretty Boy Floyd became the Robin Hood of the day as he robbed banks and sometimes paid up farm mortgages with the money.

Rev. Koch knew times were hard and social life was sparse. That's why he continued to open the parish hall on Saturday nights so he and the young men he had taught to play the violin could fill the room with fiddle music. Folks came from far and wide. Some walked. Some rode their horses. Dozens came in wagons or bobsleds pulled by old worn-out plow horses.

They came to the church to dance the evening into forgetfulness. Some of them hadn't danced since Hector was a pup but that didn't stop them. As they danced they remembered springtime in a distant land, and music and laughter that had too long been buried in depression, droughts, and plagues of grasshoppers. They needed to dance, to forget some things and remember others..

I sat in the corner tapping my toe. "*Nar,* pure foolishness," Mama remarked as Papa grabbed her by the waist and swung her around the floor until she was panting. It was a bit of heaven in a barren land to see Papa and Mama laugh and dance.

I watched the ageless soap opera unfold as the preacher matched the teenage girls in their floursack dresses with the handsome young bucks dressed in clean, worn overalls. It was glorious to see them whirl to the old Danish folk dances until they were dizzy. Sometimes I would see them sneak outside. I dreamed of being old enough to have a boy ask me to dance.

No music had ever seemed so sweet, or so needed. How I loved that pastor and the way he was trying to make the church be the church. After the old folks got tired and headed home with their sleeping broods, the young folks swung their partners to "Yankee Doodle Dandy" and "O, Dem Golden Slippers" until the sun came creeping over the hills.

But not everyone thought the dances were a wonderful thing. Some people were so on edge from the terrible economy, loneliness, and despair that they began arguing not about Danish or English or theology but about dancing. Some even said certain young folks sneaked out for home brew during the dances.

"Right here under prohibition, in the church, and under that preacher's very nose some young folks are turning into genuine criminals and drunkards!" folks argued.

"My, my," was all Papa had to say about that.

I had seen conflict at home. Now that I was desperately struggling with a need to find eternal answers, the only answers the church leaders were struggling with seemed to have nothing to do with God. They were talking in groups, shouting angrily. Those who agreed with Rev. Koch argued with those who felt it was time for a new pastor who could settle things by being more Danish . . . more English . . . more spiritual . . . more anything.

It seemed you had to choose sides, not for God or the Devil, but for or against the pastor. Uncle Emil had said, "Troublemakers spend all their time getting folks on their side so nobody ever gets on God's side."

I wanted to know why folks weren't talking about God any more at the church. How would we weather the depression without Rev. Koch and God? Who would find help to live or die if the church no longer had time to talk about God?

My world was falling apart. I had escaped conflict at home by fleeing to the Kochs' parsonage. But now God's house was crowded with the same kind of turmoil I had tried to escape.

How could they ask a man of God, who each Sunday preached God's Holy Word, who even (in my youthful imagination) looked exactiy like God, to leave? How could they put him out just when the world was falling apart and we needed to find a real God? The church had been my last resort in my search for God, but now he seemed very far away.

As things got more heated, I began to dread going to church on Sundays. At the Kochs' I had been able to exist as my own person, a valuable individual. I had belonged and truly felt at home. Now I belonged nowhere.

As things got more heated, the church seemed hostile and hateful. Mrs. Koch still played the organ but her music was not the same. Where it had once made me want to dance, now I heard a funeral dirge.

"Papa," I implored, "I can't find God in the same place I always looked for him. Where is he now? Where does he go when churches fight?"

But Papa didn't know. I wondered if Papa had found God. He had a promise to keep and he had searched so hard.

A new minister came. Rev. Koch began leading services in his home. Papa and Mama went, but nobody had any money to pay a pastor.

I didn't understand church splits and squabbling then, and I don't now. Troubles are like babies, growing larger by nursing and always yelling for a change. But those doing the yelling always want somebody else to do the changing.

How can the world model peace if churches teach folks to fight? Every Sunday, I'm told, nine million unhappy folks are walking the streets looking for a peaceful church. I believe the answer is to define the purpose of the church. If a congregation decides that *the sole purpose of the church is to seek and to save the lost and train believers for discipleship* and that any unkind word may keep someone out of heaven, it will model peace. If every church would teach this principle, I believe heaven could be filled lots sooner.

Soon we did not go to church anywhere. I was at home much more. In the past, no matter how dreary weekdays were at home, I could always stash away Sunday as a sparkling day that made up for everything. But Sunday became as difficult as any other day. So when Mama decided one summer Sunday that we would not go to church, I felt sad but it didn't matter as much as it might have before.

It was strange to stay home an entire morning and do nothing. By afternoon, the sweltering heat was replaced with an eery, foreboding saffron mustard stillness. Midnight colored clouds and the roll of distant thunder seemed to hover in almost reachable distance across the drought-ridden wheat fields.

"It's brewing a gully washer," Papa declared. "We'll milk early."

We ran through torrents of pelting rain to reach the barn. But Papa had made a grave error. This was no time to be in the barn. It was already swaying back and forth like a drunken seaman. Then the silo came crashing down. Papa's voice screamed above the mayhem, "Join hands! Don't let go of anyone's hand until we are safely in the house!"

Defiantly, he pushed against the momentum of the storm. We reached the house just as an old oak tree came crashing down behind us.

For an eternity we all sat huddled in the dismal dank basement. Through the tiny window the thunder roared and the lightning flashed. We could see our mighty oak and maples uprooted and tossed across the barnyard. Our majestic red hip roof barn stood tipsily and the silo was like a help-less child sprawled on the ground.

Even with my hand in Papa's I was much more afraid of God than of the storm. I had lied to the teacher. The church was dying. The preacher had been kicked out. Nobody had found God and now all of us in the church would be exposed to the whole world just as Miss Marcott had exposed me.

The storm was followed by an eery stillness. As we climbed out of the cellar it looked as though God had had a tantrum. The play was over, it seemed to us. The curtain had been pulled and the players were going home. A forgiving silence seemed to push away the clouds to let the brilliant, curious stars peek at the havoc God had wrought.

But the play was not over. In the darkness I could see Mr. Knudson's Model T clanking and rat-tling at full speed down the road. When he reached us he jumped from behind the wheel and screamed at the top of his voice across the soggy cow lot, "De church, she is burning! De church, she is burning!"

I was still holding Papa's hand and I wouldn't let go as Papa jumped into Knudson's car. Mama protested but Papa didn't say "No," so I went with them. We were still miles away when we spotted the flames. Lightning had struck the church; God was burning it down. I clung to Papa.

By the time we finally bumped our way over the gravel roads, it seemed the whole congrega-tion—still divided—had gathered. Those who sup-ported the preacher stood on the north lawn of the church, and those who opposed him huddled to the south. Papa wouldn't join either group. He just stood smack-dab in the middle.

Everyone watched, mesmerized, glaring at the other group as if blaming each other for what God seemed to be blaming all of us for doing.

Papa noticed it, too. "Ya, we got a real active church," he muttered under his breath. "Half are active for the preacher, half agin' him."

"Maybe God is mad at us because we built a beautiful church and left him outside," I whispered.

"Maybe God is trying to get us to stop playing games with his church," said Papa softly.

It was too late to form a bucket brigade. The flames were leaping higher than the church and the roof was caving in. Standing there in the flickering, terrifying light, holding tightly to Papa's hand, I was deathly afraid of God. All I could think of was Papa's promise. How would he keep it now?

"Papa, we barely missed being killed tonight when the oak tree fell right behind us! If we had died, where would we all be right now?"

Papa did not hear me because by now the walls were crumbling and the fire crackled loudly. Hungry flames licked up the north side. Then the south side was gone. Everyone backed into the old church yard. We were all standing together. Nobody argued. Nobody said anything. When three of the walls were down, each person slinked around in the shadows to return to his or her side of the splintered church.

I was glad Papa had spoken up at the last meeting. I knew he had been absolutely right. I whispered to him, "I don't think God gives a hoot which of his thousand languages we use, or if we dance happily in the church. I think he cares about how much we love each other and whether we tell folks how to get to heaven."

"Shhhh," said Papa. "Look at how sad everyone is. We'll talk about it on the way home."

"Da pulpit!" someone shouted. "Save it! Jes Schmidt's beautiful hand-carved pulpit. Da twelve disciples, dey is burning up!" It crashed down from its exalted place on the one remaining wall into the fire below.

The flames were ravenous. Mrs. Koch's organ was next. Never again would Beethoven's counterpoint flow through that magnificent instrument, making the angels sing in my soul.

God was no respecter of property. Those who were mad at the preacher always sat on one side, the rest of us on the other, but the flames didn't care. They greedily devoured all of the pews. Nobody would sit in any of them again.

Only the marble baptistry still stood, its ghoulish, inky silhouette defying the flames.

The final burnt offering was the majestic, towering steeple. As it teetered, the bell swung dizzily back and forth in the wind. It was tolling for the last time its own death knell.

"*En, to, tre, fira, fem, sex,*" Papa counted rapidly. But I could not count with him. I covered my ears and began crying. Who cared how long the bell had lived? Who cared that the church was split and the preacher was leaving? Who cared that the organ lay in ashes? That the music had died? Who cared that Papa had not been able to keep his promise? Some day we would die just like the music and the bell, but we would have to give an account to Jesus.

The spectacle of the bell drew everyone together again. The two factions stood side by side. For the first time in the entire drama, everyone began crying together in one voice.

"Jesus, Jesus, Jesus!"

Then I saw the flames illuminate the altar. There was Thorvaldson's crucified Jesus dying on the cross, his loving hands outstretched to the West Denmark congregation, his compassionate eyes piercing the crumbling world around us, reaching into the depths of our souls. His robes were aflame, his arms still outstretched. Above him the angels still sang in the smoky midnight of our souls.

In the shadows Papa dropped to his knees and I knelt with him.

For the first time I saw Rev. Koch and his family. They had been standing in the shadows weeping uncontrollably. Now they came and fell on their knees beside Papa and me.

The cry from the congregation continued.

"Oh, Jesus, Jesus, Jeeeessssuuuus, Jeeeessssuuuuss . . ." I couldn't tell whether people were cursing or confessing.

In the midst of the church's requiem, the bell clanged one final feeble click as it settled into its coffin of ashes.

Folks were kneeling like ghostly shadows in the brilliance of the horrendous holocaust, trying to make peace with a God I wondered if they had ever really met.

I was scared to death of God, of the church, of both living and dying. Had I foolishly put my hope in something that God would burn down to get our attention?

I had waited three years for someone to explain to me why Helga had died. I wanted to know for certain where she would spend eternity. Papa had promised we would find out, and Papa was a promise keeper. I had thought it would be easy to find God in the church, but it had been very, very hard and our search was not over yet.

The drought had burned up our crops. Every Sunday we had prayed for rain and now in the only rainstorm of the summer, God had mocked us by burning down the church.

Rev. Koch had preached, "By this sign shall all men know you are my disciples, that you love one another." Maybe the real test of God's love in us was whether we could get along with each other. Papa tried harder than anyone I had ever known. I promised God I would try as hard as I could to get along with others, too. And if that were impossible I would get out of the way of those who would not let me model peace. Let them waste their lives fussing. Surely God had something better for me to do with my life.

"Oh, Papa," I wailed unashamedly, "the church is dying!"

Papa drew me close and tried to steer me away from the ruined church, but I wouldn't budge. Every eye turned to me, but I didn't care. I wanted everyone to remember for the rest of their lives how precious the church is and how we can't play games with God. I pledged that when I grew up I would spend my life keeping the church alive so that Jesus would not have to be crucified afresh.

But the real breaking point came shortly after the church building burned to the ground. Rev. Koch was leaving West Denmark. No, he was not going to another church to share God's love. He would be working in his uncle's brick yard in Iowa.

What would he do with his stately black robe and honeycombed collar and all those wonderful sermons about love and God? Who would hear God singing through Mrs. Koch's incredible organ music? Surely he couldn't read the powerful word of God to mere bricks? Who would dance to his fiddle? Or sing the great hymns of the church? Or be lifted to God through the choir's beautiful music? Who would help people find God when the church and all our dreams lay in ashes?

As I watched the Kochs packing to move I realized I had been shielded from the hardship of the church by the church. Now I was on my own and had no church and no Rev. Koch. I had to move on. But to where? I had to talk with someone. I was sure it was too late for Papa and me to ever find God. God had burned down the church and now he had taken away our pastor. I felt guilty. I should have talked to someone while there was a church. Maybe it was all my fault. I had waited too long and God had sent Helga's death and then the fight and now the fire. I had to find Papa. I had to talk to someone.

As I traveled the woebegone ancient gravel road leading from West Denmark to where we lived I noticed that everything I saw was desiccated and dusty. Except for the one temper tantrum from heaven, it had not rained at all for three months. The ponds had long since disappeared and the pastures were brown and barren. We children had to herd the cattle along the roadsides where they could barely find enough grass to keep them alive and milking.

For seven years I had been the baby of the family, with two older brothers and two older sisters. Then in the span of four years, Mama and Papa had four new babies, two girls and two boys.

Papa was behind on the mortgage. The meager milk check would not even pay the interest on the $10,000 note. For two years there had been no rain. Then this year the grasshoppers again had found each green blade of grass that dared to lift its head toward the torrid summer sky. Worse yet, they had neatly deposited their despicable raven-black eggs each place they had devoured a stalk of wheat, dooming next year's crop.

"Hoovervilles," shanty towns of homeless people, were everywhere. Four years ago the bad kids at our little school had chanted: "Ladies and gentlemen, take my advice: Vote for Hoover, 'cause Smith's got lice." Now Hoover sat sequestered in a well-guarded White House. The streets were blocked off. Desperate veterans who had been promised they would receive a bonus in 1943 felt they could not wait that long. They were marching on Washington, D.C., demanding their bonuses *now*. They formed a veterans' village with 20,000 people living in paper boxes in Anacosta. One thousand of them stormed the capital. Washington was under siege. General MacArthur with his aides, Major George Patton and Major Dwight D. Eisenhower, were sent in with tanks to protect the president against the very men who had gone to France and Germany to protect the United States.

By 11 p.m. Anacosta was on fire. The sky was scarlet. Women and children were trapped and had to be rescued. Congress demanded to know why this action was taken against unarmed veterans. America was at its lowest ebb.

In Albany, New York, Franklin D. Roosevelt announced that Hoover had lost the election. Indeed, Roosevelt replaced Herbert Hoover in 1933 after winning in a landslide. But people threatened that unless he gave them some relief he would be the last United States president. Folks clung to their radios to listen to Roosevelt's "Fireside Chats" not knowing that the president always sat down because polio had so crippled him that he could hardly stand. Since the church had no answers, people reasoned, maybe FDR did.

At home our family had become even more polarized. Those who sided with Mama were in, the others out. My brother Mal was sent to CCC (the Civilian Conservation Corps instituted under FDR's New Deal) camp and was never to live at home again. I used a technique I have employed in every conflict throughout my life. Instead of fighting, I flee. If I can't flee, I silently take the arrows. This was also Papa's way of coping. Long ago he had fled Denmark and sought refuge in a strange new land. He had buried himself in stumps and stones and eighteen-hour days seeking forgetfulness and a new life. But America had failed him.

Papa and I had seen the church battle itself and we had not been able to save it. It had failed us or maybe, worse yet, we had failed it. We were both battle-scarred outsiders.

As I walked along that dusty country road that day, I knew I didn't belong at home and I didn't have a church. So, where could I go?

I was twelve and my county exams said I had passed from the little Pine Grove one-room school. Papa was working for the WPA (Work Progress Administration, another New Deal public works program). To have sunk that low was, in his opinion, to be much lower than fourth class. It was a disgrace he could not hide. It was even worse than a disgrace. Papa said it was illegal and it nearly destroyed him to think he had come to America to do something illegal. Grover Cleveland, who was president from 1885 to 1889 and 1893 to 1897, had said,

> I will not be a party to stealing money from one group of citizens to give it to another group of citizens no matter what the need or apparent justification. Once the coffers of the federal government are open to the public, there will be no shutting them again. It is the responsibility of the citizens to support their government. It is not the respon-

sibility of the government to support its citizens.

But Congress voted to open the coffers for the very first time in America's short history. When the Supreme Court declared it unconstitutional, the money had already been spent. FDR replaced the Supreme Court justices who opposed government relief. With no limit to the number of consecutive terms a president could serve, it was a matter of outliving those who opposed public assistance.

Papa's conscience made him work doubly hard on WPA jobs so he could feel he earned his money, but sometimes it seemed like he was only doing make work. Some of the work was excellent, such as building parks and roads. Sometimes, however, he was told to dig holes that others were ordered to fill up. When Papa read that sixty million dollars had been given in revenues to farmers, the unemployed, the sick, and sometimes the merely lazy, he knew that welfare was entrenched and irrevocable. He predicted that someday it would bankrupt America.

As I walked along that road on that sweltering day knowing Papa was on WPA and knowing how humiliating it was for him, I thought about his dreams for a new world. I thought of Rosa and Mama and of Mama's dreams of being first class. I thought about the church fighting its pastor and each other. I thought of God shouting "STOP" and burning down the church building,and Rev. Koch working in a brick yard instead of preaching from a hand-carved pulpit. I thought of an armed America pointing guns at the veterans who had fought the war to end all wars.

No, there absolutely could not be a God!

Chapter Ten

"Vel, of Course!"

*D*eep in thought I saw the dust rising on the road. The day was insufferably hot, the ground unbearably dry and the road ahead of me uncertain. That is when God taught me a lesson that has stayed with me in long years of ministry: In every dry and barren desert, God has streams of fresh, living water. Count on it!

The model A Ford that came chugging by belonged to Rev. B. Emil Nielson, pastor of the tiny Baptist church in Milltown. He was a Danish immigrant with very little command of the English language, $400 a year in salary if the Danish Conference and the church could pay him (which it usually couldn't), a tiny ramshackle parsonage and kids to raise.

God's angel riding in a Model A Ford? I did not see the angel wings or hear God's trumpets sounding. However, if I had not been so angry with God, I might have. What I did see was a sweltering, dusty country preacher, mopping his brow and saying with a great, warm smile, "You vant a ride, young lady?"

Kids were not afraid to ride with strangers in those days. And no one who had the luxury of a car and enough gas to run it would think of passing up anyone who was walking.

No one walked for exercise. I had walked four miles to and from school for eight years. All the kids did. Walking for exercise was *nar* (plum foolishness). You walked to get where you were going. You walked because you couldn't afford a horse or wagon. You walked because God had given you two strong legs and you had better well thank God you could.

"I'm da preacher from de Baptist church! Vare is you heading?"

Where was I heading? I had one extra dress and one pair of shoes, and they had newspaper in the soles to keep out the dirt. I was walking to visit my father who had sunk so low he was working on the WPA. Those who could afford to look down on anyone who was on relief called the Works Project Administration "We Putter Around." Nobody mentioned that their Papa worked there. It was the last stop before the poor house.

All my life I shall remember that though that day seemed the darkest day of my life it was really the tunnel leading to the light that would

change my entire world. No seminary course, nor
the several degrees I was to earn later, would be
as valuable in my ministry as the lessons I learned
that day. Was not Jesus hungry with the hungry?
Homeless with the homeless? Lonely with the
lonely? Scourged and bruised with all of wounded,
hurting humanity? I have thanked Almighty God
over and over, as he has called me to work with
his wounded children, for that course in compassion and love and getting involved to the point of
inconvenience taught by Pastor Nielson on that
parched summer day.

After talking to me for five minutes Pastor
Nielson understood the problem: I needed a home.
Without hesitation he offered a seven-word solution: "Vel, ve vil yust go see Mary!" No social workers, federal government programs, or charity. Just
the Samaritan traveling along the roadside, seeing a need and filling it.

We chugged along in silence. A thousand
thoughts flew through my mind. I had been questioning God and I was sure that was a sin. Now I
was frightened because I knew God had heard me
or he wouldn't have sent a preacher. He could have
sent anyone. Why a preacher?

I had just left one parsonage and now I was
about to enter another one, far less commodious,
much more meager—but filled with the same Rev.
Koch spirit. Mary Nielson must have attended the
same school of life. Her astute evaluation of my
situation and response to my needs were summed
up in just three words of broken English, the
sweetest words I had ever heard: "Vel, of course!"

No government agency gave a psychological examination. There was no evaluation of the soundness of such a financial undertaking. She did not wonder where she would put another bed in her tiny parsonage or question how she would feed another mouth. Just three words: "Vel, of course!"

I decided then and there that if there were a God and if he would let me know him, for the rest of my life I would be a "vel of course" Christian. Little did I know how rich I became that day! At every crossroad in my life God had put an angel—Papa, Rev. Koch, and now the Nielsons.

Looking back I realize that it took me less than ten minutes to learn that the Nielsons were purpose driven. Their purpose was to live so close to God that everyone in Milltown would go to heaven. No price was too dear! No involvement was too inconvenient! No outreach was too risky! No love was withheld! I was the wounded one along life's Jericho road. It was only natural that they would bind my wounds. How else could they show me the way to heaven?

"Ve vil go out to see your Papa," Pastor Nielson suggested. No nonsense. We would just go.

And so we did. Dear wonderful Papa who had never been able to give Mama first class. Poor Papa, who some thought had never measured up although I knew he had been first class all along! Papa had tears in his eyes when Pastor Nielson told him they had plenty of house and heart room. Poor Papa who had searched for God and never found him! Now on this WPA job, the lowest he could have sunk, he saw a light at the end of the tunnel. Maybe there was a God and maybe God had been watching over all those he loved when he had been doing his best but his best had not been good enough. Maybe it took God's best to make it good enough.

Now Pastor Nielson had won the right to say, "Ve is hafing revival in de church tonight. You and the missus should come."

Papa did not promise. He would never lie. I knew if Papa had said "yes" he would be there. But he just said, "Ve vil see."

Papa was groping for an understanding of the church, not sure he was ready to take another plunge. I understood how he felt. At that moment, I loved Papa more than I had ever dreamed I could love anyone. WPA didn't matter. Pending farm foreclosure didn't matter. Years of struggle and conflict didn't matter. Papa had *not* given up. He had said, "Ve vil see." Because Pastor Nielson lived so close to God he had made my Papa willing to try God one last time.

That night at the supper table I was reluctant to eat. The one not-too-big bowl on the table held boiled potatoes and pork rind. I had learned that the Nielsons ate whatever the farmers might send to their back door. They lived on faith and love. I had not eaten all day but this time we had no cow to give the minister, as when I had gone to the Kochs.

So I took one tiny potato. I knew I had nothing to offer but need.

"Eat up, Rosa. The Lord gives food to the hungry," Pastor Nielson said, quoting Psalm 146:7 as he piled my plate high with potatoes and then gave me his lump of butter. Full of warm and loving generosity, he reached over and patted my hand and said, "Vel, Rosa, now you just don't have to vorry about nuttin' any more."

"I'm not worried about where I will sleep tonight," I quietly replied.

Pastor Nielson was a no-nonsense, practical preacher. He knew he had done his homework. He had gotten involved to the point of inconvenience, thus earning the right to ask me the question Papa and I had struggled with so long and hard, a question I was to ask hundreds of people later: "Vat is you vorried about?"

My heart spilled out! My reservation was gone! My hour had come! *This man must have the answer,* I thought. *And I must know it.* "I'm worried about where I would go if I died," I blurted out, my tears spilling over.

Because the food was all gone and his children were clamoring for his attention, he wisely deferred the answer. "Come to church tonight," he said, "and ve vill show you how you can belong to the family of God."

The family of God? Family of God! I, who had never really felt a part of any family . . . if I could belong to the family of God I would permanently have a family . . . a real family. It sounded like a banana split with chocolate, strawberry, and butterscotch sauce and whipped cream and nuts and a cherry on the top. (I had seen this food for angels in the drugstore once and vowed that when I was rich I would really buy one.)

The one-room country church where Pastor Nielson's flock gathered was not elegant like the West Denmark or Askov churches. It boasted only a bare plank floor, a tiny wooden homemade pulpit, an out-of-tune piano, and a novice piano player—quite a contrast to Mrs. Koch's elegant organ music. There was no Thorvaldson statue of Jesus with outstretched arms and piercing eyes that enfolded you in love. There were just wooden plank pews and Pastor Nielson's preaching.

He told how everyone had sinned. God couldn't have sinners in heaven because then there would be depression and riots and prisons and people fighting, making heaven no different from earth. Since everyone has sinned, none are righteous and fit for heaven.

"God is a loving God," the pastor continued in his melodic Danish brogue. "God wanted everyone in heaven, but man's sin had shut him out of heaven. God is a just God and he has to punish sin.

"This was God's dilemma: How could sinners go to heaven? How could he have a heaven without sin if he allowed sinners to get in? Somehow He had to get rid of the sin before mankind was fit for heaven."

Goodness, that is what Papa and I have struggled with all these years, I thought.

My eyes were glued on Pastor Nielson. He did not wear a long black robe and a honeycombed collar. He was not proclaiming God's word from an intricately carved pulpit. His old black serge suit was threadbare and shone at the elbows. He was bald, not tall, dark and handsome like Rev. Koch. And yet, there was something exactly the same about these two men of God: their compassion for me and their willingness to risk themselves to prove it. Yes, God must be alive, if I could just find him. How I wished Papa were here.

Chapter Eleven

Fifteen Inches
from Jesus

*T*he gentle country preacher was not pounding the pulpit or waving his arms and shouting. His voice was soft and sincere with the melodic accent of Papa's fatherland. His face revealed his profound character and purpose. This man of God didn't waste time beating around the bush, yet he did not seem fanatical or overbearing.

He lifted his three middle fingers to represent the three men dying on crosses on a lonely Calvary hill. I leaned forward as though life and death depended on what he was saying, which, as I was soon to find out, it did!

"When de wonderful loving Good Lord died on de cross, he died between two of the worstest crooks in de world. This one went to heaven," he said dramatically, "and this . . . one . . . CHOSE eternal hell. And in between those two sinners hung the sinless Jesus," he continued, lifting his middle finger high, "dying . . . for . . . both of the sinners . . . both of them." He punctuated it with ever so gentle a staccato.

In the stillness a summer storm was gathering. In the waning twilight it seemed an eternity before the next words came out.

"One thief turned to Jesus and said, 'Remember me when you come into your kingdom.' One thief ruled him out and was forever and eternally lost."

What a dumb mistake, I reasoned. *Jesus would have wasted his whole life on earth if he were wrong. But if he were right that thief was wasting a whole eternity.*

This was no phoney, sloppy sentimentalism. This was a clear explanation coming from a battle-scarred warrior who put his life on the line for what he knew was true. Pastor Nielson was like David battling the giant Goliath, Daniel in the lion's den, or Gideon marching in a battle for the souls of men!

"Now vasn't dat the vorld's saddest mistake—to be dying and to be just fifteen inches from God's Son who was offering forever and ever in heaven . . . and . . . then to . . . miss it?"

The pastor was not just preaching theology—he was painting a picture so vivid, so perfectly clear that no one could misunderstand. I had never rejected God. Why would anyone do such a stupid thing? I had searched for him but never found him. Papa had been searching, too. We had been on a long pilgrimage, searching with all our hearts.

Then the pastor painted the crucifixion. I sat there thinking it through. *They nailed Him to a cross with great huge nails like those Papa used on the farm . . . as if he were even lower than fourth class. Not even his disciples, who should have been his best friends, were there. The man at the pool and the lame and blind men—where were they when Jesus needed them?*

Jesus was desperately lonely. I am desperately lonely. Just think of it! If only I knew him we could be best friends. All he was asking was cool clear water . . . and they gave him vinegar. My mouth was dry. I wanted to go for water, to give it to Jesus . . . to take him off the cross and stop the sky from turning black.

It was just Jesus and me—and my heart was breaking. There were no dramatics, no elegant oratory, no hand-carved altar, no marble Thorvaldson Jesus with the nail-pierced hands and the loving eyes beckoning sinners, no black robes, no wonderful organ music. There was just a simple country preacher whose call was so crystal-clear he could do nothing else. And, there was Jesus and me!

This Jesus was the one Papa and I had searched for through death, discord, and depression. This Jesus was alive! He was for real. And he was for ME! I could almost hear Jesus cry to a Father who had forsaken him because he could not look at MY sin. I had done that to Jesus. I had nailed him there.

My heart was bursting. It seemed there was no one in church but just Jesus and me and I had to do something about ME. I wanted to go to him, to tell him how terribly sorry I was, and then make them take him down.

Deliberately and with sterling sincerity Pastor Nielson explained the innocent dying for the guilty, the just for the unjust, so simply, so beautifully, so lovingly that any child—like me—could not possibly misunderstand.

Pastor Nielson used an illustration about Billy Jones. Murderers were mighty rare back then in rural Wisconsin. When Billy Jones got drunk one night, when there was no food in the house and the children were barefoot and the farm was being sold at auction and his wife began nagging, he went berserk and wiped the whole dismal depression from his whiskey-soaked mind by killing his wife and his daughter together.

"It's like this," Pastor Nielson explained, "I didn't do what Billy Jones done. And Billy Jones is gonna die for what he did do. Now since I am innocent and if I vould be villing to die for Billy Jones and the law said that was OK and Billy Jones said it was OK, then Billy Jones could go free even though he vas guilty and I vould die even though I am not. All Billy Jones vould have to do is to agree to let me die for him. Forever after that he could go scot free."

His three fingers were still lifted high. The kerosene lamps in the window were flickering. Suddenly it seemed I saw Jesus—magnificent, strong, and masculine, much more beautiful than the statue on the West Denmark altar. He was alive and looking down at me with his wonderfully compassionate eyes and reaching to me with his loving nail-pierced hands. Yes, now I was dead sure Papa and I were the two thieves hanging on either side of Jesus.

"This here one thief, he knew a good thing ven he saw it," Pastor Nielson continued. "He just begged Jesus if he vould take all his sins . . . all the murder and killing and stealing he had done! Could he just unload them on Jesus? And just to prove that you don't get to heaven by being good, or being baptized, or going to church, or giving offerings but just by accepting him as your substitute, Jesus told him right straight out that he vould be the first one he vould take to heaven with him. Sure, he probably vould have done lots of good things to thank Jesus if he had lived, but he didn't need it to get to heaven. All he had to do was to accept Jesus as his substitute."

One lamp sputtered. It was out of kerosene. The sun had set and a murky darkness was creeping over the summer night. The wind was blowing branches of an old elm tree against the barren windowpanes. The rain began to pelt the sky, thunder rolled, and lightning flashed.

Now the pastor pointed to the finger on the left. "Isn't it a shame. This criminal vas dying just fifteen inches from Jesus, and he said he'd take his chances." Lightning flashed as bright as pure daylight. I felt like God was talking out loud to me. Crash! Bang! Thunder rolled, the little church shook and I shook. But nothing shook Pastor Nielson. He was battling Satan and he knew it. He just kept on preaching as if God himself were talking right through him.

"That thief just said, 'Save yourself, Jesus, if you're the Son of God.'"

Fifteen inches from Jesus! Why, I felt as though I were fifteen inches from Jesus. I felt closer to finding him than I had since Helga died. My quest was coming to an end. But I still didn't know how to choose him.

I wished Papa were here to help me. What if I missed God again? What if Papa never heard about God like this? I would send Pastor Nielson tomorrow to tell Papa what Jesus had done all free and clear.

Now Pastor Nielson, an ancient, worn Bible in hand, reached down to me from the little handmade pulpit, right through to my very soul. His kind, loving eyes now seemed very familiar, like those I had seen somewhere else. Then I remembered the statue of Jesus on the high altar of the Askov church the stormy night I fell in love with the church. And the Jesus on the West Denmark altar. Pastor Nielson didn't look a bit like that Jesus . . . but somehow he did.

Hands outstretched toward us sinners, Bible in hand, he was pointing to a scripture and punctuating every word with passion.

"He that BELIEVES on the SON OF GOD *has* EVERLASTING LIFE and he that BELIEVES NOT *SHALL NOT* see life but the wrath of God abides on him. John three-thirty-six."

And now the pianist was playing softly while God was orchestrating his spectacular lightning fireworks and his thunder roared an encore. Crash! Bang! Crash! I felt warm and secure inside the church. No elements could destroy me when I was this close to God.

"If you want to be in the family of God, just come to the altar. Take Jesus! He is free for all! But you have to choose him," Pastor Nielson implored.

Altar? I didn't see an altar. There wasn't even the carved pulpit with the twelve disciples—nothing that looked remotely like the altars I had seen in the Askov and West Denmark churches. The only thing up front was the pulpit, which was really an old homemade music stand, and a bare floor. That couldn't be an altar. Where was I supposed to go to find him? If only Papa were here we would do it together.

Then a frightening thought occurred to me. This must be the first time anyone in this room had ever heard how to get to heaven. If the people here had known all this they would surely have told me and everyone else in this room. And since they must have never heard, then they must all be wanting to come to that altar just like me. If I didn't get there soon, there might not be any room for me. I had to find that altar quickly!

"Just come and kneel right here," he said, his finger pointing to the well-worn floor in front of him. *So,* I thought, *That must be what an altar looks like in a Baptist Church. Just a bare plank floor.* It sounded funny but who was I to ask questions when heaven was at stake?

My heart spilled over in great joyous tears of serendipity. My long journey was ending. I was coming home. I was going to be part of a real family—God's family. I was going to know what I would have told Helga if I had only known. My sins were forgiven, and I could know it for sure. The preacher had said, "He that believes *has* eternal life"—not "maybe" or "perhaps." Thunder boomed and the lightning made the church a cathedral.

As much as I loved God's church, as close as I was to God, I would never have asked for another miracle. But as I knelt there alone, just me and God, I felt a strong familiar arm encircling me. In the brilliant light of God's wonderful fireworks, *I looked up into the weeping eyes of Papa!*

I did not know he had come late and taken a seat in the back. *Papa came to church because he loves me,* I thought. *He is coming because the preacher offered me his home.*

But I was wrong. Those may be some of the reasons Papa came to church that night, but they weren't the reasons he was weeping at the altar. Papa was coming for himself, coming to accept Jesus . . . coming home.

I remembered a story Rev. Koch had told about a man walking all alone carrying a huge load down a weary road. A farmer comes along in his wagon and offers the traveler a lift. He gets in the wagon but leaves the load on his back.

"Take it off," says his benefactor.

"Oh, no sir. I couldn't ask you to carry both me and my load," the man replies.

I had never understood that story until now. I forgot there was anybody in the church but Papa and me. Just us two, walking along life's road with a heavy load and Jesus coming along to both lift our load and take us home.

Papa's heavy shoulders shook and I realized he was sobbing great belly sobs. It seemed he was weeping away the heavy loads of all his years, of Rosa, of all he hadn't been able to give Mama, of stumps and stones and grasshoppers and Wisconsin blizzards and the whole wretched depression.

It seemed as if the load he had so gallantly carried for years had finally crushed him. It isn't the size of the dragon in the fight but the size of the fight in the dragon. Papa had fought dragons gallantly for too long. Tonight he was surrendering it all. It was as if he had carried all alone a load big enough for six men and tonight he was laying it down and asking for help. Papa had never given up on anything before in his life and never asked anyone for help. But tonight it seemed he needed help and had found it. Someone much bigger had come along to carry the heavy end.

"If only someone had told us long ago, how different life would have been for you, Rose," Papa whispered through his tears.

"And for you, Papa."

I was home. Papa was home . . . in God's family. I was in love—my first love—with Jesus. I would always serve him. Never again would I have to wonder where I would spend eternity.

Pastor Nielson prayed a simple prayer with us and we repeated it: "Dear Jesus, I know I am a sinner. I know I can't save myself. I know you died on the cross for me. I take you as my substitute, my Savior, and I make you the Lord of my life. And for all the rest of my life, I will tell others how they can know they have eternal life also. Thank you for making me a child of God."

That night I gave away my entire life—and found one much better because it was abundant life, life for now and forever.

Before I rose from my knees I had promised I would be a missionary. It was not an impetuous decision but the beginning of a lifelong commitment. No one ever gets lost on a straight road, and I was on that straight road with Jesus. I would live among the Hottentots and gladly suffer and die in some forgotten jungle. Anything, Lord! Anything! If true wisdom comes from learning to discern the difference between the passing and the eternal in our lives, that night I received more wisdom than all my academic studies in later years would ever offer.

I never did get to Africa. God was opening up another mission field for me. My call was to take the gospel to the country that needed it most.

I was only twelve, but I was called of God and I had answered God's call and I would never again be able to escape that crystal clear direction for my life. I knew that until the day I die, whenever and wherever I see another hurting child, a Rose . . . or a Papa . . . another lost soul, I would explain just exactly what Jesus had done for me and what he would do for them. With God helping me, I had no other choice. Period!

For 45 years of ministry that call has always been in the inner recesses of my heart, a security even in the darkest night that I am his and he is mine. Through death of loved ones or despair of circumstances or discord in the world, I have never been able to deny that call. It has always been there to get me joyfully back on track. As Jesus set his face like flint to Calvary, so my course was finally and firmly set in the concrete of God's purpose for my life.

"Papa, you really are a promise keeper," I said quietly. Great men might come and go but I knew Papa would always be my hero. That's the test of a real Papa.

"It has been a long road," Papa articulated softly through his tears, his arm securely around me. "Now the rest of the promise we made is to make sure others don't have to search so hard to find him as we did. From now on, everyone we meet must know about Jesus."

I knew Papa would keep that promise, too, until the end of time. And he did.

The folks had all left the church and it was just Papa and me—and God. The preacher knew we needed some time together. We got off our knees and sat in one of the old plank pews. We just sat there for a long time while the kerosene lamps flickered in the semidarkness. We listened to the wind brushing the lilac bushes and the willows against the window and the rain dripping from the eaves. It felt like the Fourth of July when the parade was over, the marching band had gone home and the fireworks were over. The warm memories of the wonderful celebration would last forever.

The storm was abating. In those days the last person to leave the church was expected to blow out the lights and close the door. Papa would walk the five miles back to home. I would walk next door to the parsonage. We stood there looking at the murky sky. The old half-eaten piece of green cheese called the moon was coming out in a buttermilk sky. I was glad Papa would not have to walk home in the rain.

"Thanks for coming, Papa. You've always been there when I needed you most," I said as I hugged Papa's waterlogged shoulders once more.

"It vas nothing."

But Pastor Nielson must have thought it was. He had waited all that time to take my rain-soaked Papa home in his old Model A. I never forgot that lesson. Evangelism is walking the extra mile!

Later that night, snug on a little army cot in a corner of the parsonage, I couldn't go to sleep thinking of what God and I and Papa had done. I was only twelve, but I was called of God and I would never be able to forget that call.

I learned more about pastoral care from Pastor Nielson's preaching that winter than I would later learn from seminary training and five degrees. He said, "When an archer misses the mark, he looks for the fault within himself. Failure to hit the bull's-eye is never the fault of the target. To improve your aim, improve yourself."

I wrote these things in a little black book.

Chapter Twelve

Growing and Stretching

*P*apa and I were baptized in Little Butternut Lake on a crystal clear sparkling sun-filled Sunday morning. We were dunked all the way under. Pastor Nielson told me that it was a symbol that my sins were all gone and we were rising to a new life. No halfway sprinkling for him.

Mama and my siblings were also baptized. All of our concerns at home were not settled, but the sin question clearly was.

I had never been happier. The birds were singing, the sun was shining, and Papa and I had our sins forgiven.

I was going on thirteen. Since I had passed my county exams I was ready to leave the little Pine Grove one-room country school. I wanted to go to high school but this seemed impossible until the

Nielsons said I could live with them and attend the high school in town that winter.

But Papa didn't like the idea of being beholden to the preacher, especially since he was having second thoughts about working for the WPA. There was clearly something different about him now that he was a Christian. When he went back to his WPA job the day after he was baptized he hated it. As a newborn Christian, he felt he had seen life through a dull glass before. Now the sunlight was pouring into every dark corner of his life.

Mama didn't understand it. Jobs were hard to come by. Why not be glad you had one? He said there is no right way to do a wrong thing. The WPA might be all right for some people but for him it was dead wrong. He turned in his shovel and told them he didn't become a United States citizen to be a burden or to break the law.

That night he came to the Nielsons' back door and told us his decision before he went home and told Mama. I was so glad he had his faith. He would need it. I have never seen him in a greater quandary. Pastor Nielson prayed with him and Papa left with a new lilt in his step. It was as if he were on an adventure with his new faith.

Pastor Nielson gave Papa a little New Testament and underlined Romans 15:13, which says, "May the God of hope fill you with all joy and peace as you trust in him, so that you may overflow with hope by the power of the Holy Spirit." Pastor Nielson said we need hope for living far more than for dying. Dying is easy work compared to living. Dying is a moment's transition, while living is a transaction of years. He said hope makes great men. It is the poor man's income.

All that night I heard Pastor Nielson talking to people on the phone trying to find work for Papa. He told the hardware man, who was a Christian, how Papa could fix anything with almost nothing. It taught me a great lesson. It is not enough for a pastor to talk about caring. It has to be proven. A pastor needs to be unemployed with the unemployed.

When I was teaching in a college and jobs were very scarce, I used to make hundreds of calls for my students. I recall a brilliant student who was getting married in the spring. She was graduating and desperately wanted the only job open near her future husband's assignment.

I called the principal of the school where she had applied. He told me they had 38 applicants and had narrowed it down to three. One was a hometown girl they almost had to hire. However, if my student could be at the school 100 miles away at eight o'clock the next morning before they had to make the decision, he would consider her.

She had no car and no way to get there. The principal heard me say, "You can take my car, Karen." She came back the next day with the contract in hand. The school board had said that if a professor had enough faith in her to lend her a car, then she must be good. She did not let us down. She was a superb teacher and I never regretted repaying the favor done to Papa long ago.

Papa was indeed the very best carpenter and fixer in Polk county. The depression had left lots of things that needed fixing and nothing with which to fix them. Papa tackled every job with gusto, found a spare part here and there and kept the wolf away from the door at least temporarily. It wasn't long until he didn't need a pastor to find him a job, even in the midst of the depression. He proved that if you build a better mousetrap the world will indeed beat a path to your door.

He saved every cent for the mortgage. With what little crop we harvested it looked hopeful that we could hang on to the farm, even though every farm around us was gone.

Some folks were foolishly talking about how good Germany had it. America could have learned much from what was happening in Europe as war clouds cast their ominous shadows across our ocean, but many people didn't want to learn the truth. Adolph Hitler seemed to have been the answer to Germany's depression. He was offering Germany pie in the sky—they would be number one in the world with a pure Aryan race, prosperity, no Jews and jobs for everyone. An army of youth goose-stepped into the *Mein Kampf* dogma. Step, march, step! Out with God, in with prosperity and a new world order. In Italy, as the churches were dying, Mussolini was marshalling his forces singing much the same uplifting song of hope.

But at home, that simple little one-room country church was aglow with God's power. I learned that what others said could not be done *would* be done by someone who dared to believe God. All you have to do is dream dreams so impossible that you are bound to fail unless God pulls you through. I was going to need those lessons badly come spring.

It seemed trouble was coming in bunches. Papa stopped by the parsonage one day to talk with Pastor Nielson. His ashen countenance and the letter in his hand from the bank told me it had happened. It all spelled one word: "foreclosure."

It looked to me like we had nothing but God to hang on to and I wasn't quite sure that would be enough. I'm glad I got to see Papa handle this challenge firsthand. I learned faith and courage which has lasted me a lifetime—through death, misunderstandings, and 45 years of ministry. If success is measured not so much by the position one has reached as the obstacles one has overcome, then Papa was a roaring success. He had enough faith for us both, enough to accept the impossible, to do without the indispensable, and to bear the intolerable. He believed that God not only could, but that he would. That was the thing that kept Papa from running out of cope.

The little money he earned from selling the rest of the meager crops was put on a small farm in Hudson. But before he could move there a cyclone hit the farm. He had not been able to buy insurance and the house and barn were destroyed.

He had lost his money, but Papa was undaunted. Nobody can make you lose your faith without your consent. He had six months before he had to move off the farm. He was up before sunup and went to bed long after dark but in that short time he earned enough for a small down payment on a little truck farm near St. Paul.

The day I saw my family with all their belongings packed on the truck, I knew I had come to the end of an era. I was nearly thirteen and on my own.

I thought I had lost my laughter, but laughter has no foreign accent. The Nielsons laughed. They laughed joyously at the miracles God performed each day. They laughed when we made do with nothing but potatoes for supper. Poverty didn't seem to bother them.

Somehow it never entered my mind that they were poor. They pointed out how rich I was to have Papa and that life is tragic for those who have plenty to live on and nothing to live for. You take life like it is, but you don't leave it that way. The Nielsons hadn't taken me in to let me rust. Just as they had turned the tide of my life, now every act of mine must turn the tide for someone else.

My shoes were falling off my feet and I needed ink to write a composition, but nobody had any money. I handed in the composition written in pencil and put newspapers over the holes in my one pair of shoes. I knew I should be paying to stay with the Nielsons so I cleaned the house, minded the babies, worked in the garden, and helped them do work for shut-ins who needed to have their sidewalks shoveled or their houses cleaned.

My faith experienced a growth spurt the day they took me with them to a conference with just enough gas to get there and ten dollars to get back. On the way they remembered a family who needed their ten dollars for groceries. I wondered how we would get home. They were not surprised at all when Pastor Nielson was given a $10 honorarium to fill in for a speaker who became ill just before the service. It seemed as natural as breathing in and breathing out to depend on God.

They taught me ways to keep dissension out of the church. For example, an elderly tailor who was the butt of jokes in town cleaned the church for one dollar a week. His duties included bringing a bucket of water and a dipper to each service or meeting.

At one board meeting there were more young people than adults. The young people, as a joke, cast write-in votes to elect him pianist, in place of the regular pianist who had played for years. Thinking they were making fun of him, the old tailor was furious.

Pastor Nielson simply passed out the paper again so that the regular pianist, Stella, could be elected. Meanwhile, Mrs. Nielson went to the kitchen, found a candle and put it in a cake she had baked for refreshments. We then sang happy birthday to the tailor. It wasn't his birthday, but he was an old bachelor who hadn't had a birthday party in years. He wept his way through the party. From then on he cleaned the church for free, because he had seen the pure light of Jesus shining through that party.

Yes, through each experience God was molding me for ministry.

Nielson had come from Denmark with nothing but a call to serve God. He had come to go to seminary but instead he was just in time to be drafted for World War I.

As he fought in the trenches of France and saw his comrades fall one by one, he felt God's call on his life even more strongly. He had been unwilling to fight and die without thinking through what caused that war. He paraphrased George Santayana when he concluded, "He who does not learn from history is bound to repeat it."

The winter was fast coming to a close. On a blustery snowbound day when the schools were closed, when all of life was bound by three feet of snow, that simple Baptist preacher gathered the young people together for an unusual lesson. With an urgency I had seldom seen, almost as though he were a man who was drowning, he tutored us the entire day.

He started with the time of Christ. The Romans' affluence had given them so much idle time that it took greater and greater thrills to satisfy the lust of the aristocrats. The lust peaked with the bloodthirsty games such as throwing Christians to the lions in the Colosseum.

Pastor Nielson painted the Appian Way aflame with the blood of martyrs who dared to die for their faith. So vivid was his picture of those heroic Christians that I envied them and wondered if I could be like them. He said some day we may be called to be martyrs. Finally Nero ordered that no more Christians be thrown to the lions because "They die too gloriously." Those who watched them were so drawn to Christ that they became Christians.

The Romans eventually degraded into a nation of welfare recipients who were easily overrun by the barbarians. The barbarians developed into a highly productive society but then became so immoral and decadent that they had no respect for God or for any ethnic group. Even the church became corrupt, selling indulgences and sending out crusaders to slaughter other people in the name of God. These were truly the Dark Ages.

Like the weeping prophet of old, Nielson proclaimed doom for the lands which forget God: "The blood of the martyrs is always the seed of the church. To change the world we must be willing to risk more than others think safe, care more than others think wise, dream more than others think practical, expect more than others think possible."

He expounded on Martin Luther nailing his theses on the door of the Wittenberg cathedral. Then Pastor Nielson painted a vivid mental picture of Hubmaier being drowned in the Danube for his faith.

"But then Europe forgot God," that simple scholar continued. "The churches built during the great Reformation became empty and abandoned. I fought in the trenches in France in the war to end all wars. Many of my comrades lie in Flanders Field. And yet, just a few years later, history is repeating itself."

There was an urgency in his voice as he warned us about that new leader, Adolph Hitler, who had come into power as Reich Chancellor in January 30 of 1933. Hitler thundered that all Jews stood for ugliness, decay, and syphilis. They were cockroaches whose smell was the stench of Germany. They had to be destroyed. Hitler was reaching the masses with a powerful new medium—the radio. During all this, the churches, once bulwarks of justice, stood empty and silent, oblivious to human suffering.

In southern Europe, Benito Mussolini was filling the vacuum left by an impotent Roman church. Pastor Nielson predicted that unless the church became the church, this would be the most violent and savage half-century of horror and atrocity in universal history. He was confident the disaster Hitler advocated for the Jews would be an impossibility except for the seemingly anesthetized churches of Europe.

Then he warned us, "If ever America lets her churches die, she will go the way of Europe. We are now number one in technology, education, science, medicine, family, and faith. If ever we deny God we will be number one in crime, violence, illiteracy, and divorce."

Listening to him I realized that the world is never changed by accident. It is always the result of a deep faith, high intention, and daring vision. We cannot always direct the winds, but the church can adjust the sails. None of us can change the whole world but by God's grace each of us and each church can change our little corners.

We had an enormous youth group at Pastor Nielson's church. Looking back I see now how many from that group went around the world proclaiming God's word.

During this time I received many insights I would need in years to come and would pass on to generations yet unborn. The Nielsons taught me to open the church for the lost or needy, that time is all we have and we have mighty little of that, so redeem each opportunity to reach out.

I was learning by example about love as I watched their marriage. They were married not just for better or for worse, but for good.

Their purpose in ministry was soul winning, and they did it with happiness. They never seemed stressed. They were just doing something they greatly loved. Confucius said, "He who chooses a work he loves will never have to work a day in his life." I realized God would never call me to something which was not a joy. I was so right. The parsonage was a place of happiness and I prayed that some day I could be so fortunate as my hosts.

Hardly a day went by that the grocer, the homeless hobo at the door, a child or a family losing their livelihood, a young couple coming to take the big step into marriage did not find Jesus Christ. Winning souls was as normal for the Nielsons as breathing in and breathing out.

They taught me that when faced with a difficult task, act as though it is impossible to fail. If you're going after Moby Dick, take along the tartar sauce. Attempt something so impossible that you are bound to fail unless God bails you out.

These lessons were not taught—they were caught by example. The Nielsons' faith was contagious. I learned that if faith can't always move mountains, it ought at least to climb them. They had a faith that did not shrink when washed in the waters of affliction and adversity.

Some people succeed because they find greener pastures. The Nielsons stayed where they were and succeeded because they found greener people. When other pastors complained about empty churches, Pastor Nielson said, "Vel, then there must just be that many more people outside needing Jesus."

I watched them win that community . . . one by one. The Nielsons could no more keep silent about their faith than I could fly to the moon. It is hard for the Lord to guide a person who hasn't made up his or her mind which way to go. The Nielsons knew where they were going. By the end of that winter, my call was deeply entrenched as a way of life for me.

Spring came and the depression made pastors' salaries almost obsolete. The Nielsons did not need another mouth to feed. I knew that God had placed me there to send me out to use what I had learned.

Chapter Thirteen

On My Own

M ama thought I was grown up and could be on my own. These were lean days at home. Papa's little truck farm kept him working from morning until night weeding vegetables in the damp peat moss. I helped him that summer, rising at four in the morning to weed the long rows of vegetables which were sold in August. The peat made us itch and the sun baked us but I had two months all alone with Papa.

He made Mama promise that if I worked all summer I could stay home and go to high school in the fall. But by August he was totally crippled with arthritis from the long hours on his knees in the damp peat soil. We barely got the produce to market and sold. Every cent he and Mama could scrape together was needed for those still at home.

They didn't need another mouth to feed, so Mama got an idea. She had read in the St. Paul newspaper that a family wanted a maid and would pay one dollar a week. The ad suggested there was a possibility that if they liked me, I could work there and go to school in the fall. Mama called the number in the paper and told them I knew a lot more than I did. She must have been convincing because they agreed to hire me.

She put me on the bus to the Twin Cities with a whole five dollars. I had always thought that when I grew up I would visit Centralia which was 30 miles away. Now I was in a city 50 times as big and ten times further away. I was thoroughly petrified.

There turned out to be five unmarried sons in the family that hired me. Their house had 20 rooms. My room was an unfinished third-story attic. The summer of 1935 was a scorcher, with temperatures over 100 degrees day in and day out.

I had never used electricity, much less seen a vacuum cleaner or an electric washing machine. I didn't know what sounds these things made. When the vacuum cleaner came on with a roar I was sure I had broken it and would be fired. I wasn't the bill of goods Mama had sold them. I bluffed and learned as fast as I could and prayed I wouldn't be put out on the street.

I got up at four o'clock to get everything ready for breakfast, and turned in at nine. I made a lot of dumb mistakes. Thousands of people were out of work and I was amazed that with my inexperience I kept the job.

And then I learned that being fired was not the worst thing that could happen to me. The five sons were all unmarried, in their teens or twenties, and much too worldly wise. I felt relatively safe when the parents were home. But when they were gone and I was all alone in the house the sons seemed to assume that my one dollar a week salary covered their rights to do as they pleased.

Rev. Koch had said, "God has something special for someone who saves something special for somebody special." I knew that with God I was his first class citizen. Deep in my heart was a dream that one day God might let me marry a minister like Rev. Koch. I would never let the Devil destroy that possibility and vision.

After work I would lock myself in my room, fall asleep exhausted, and wake to another day of blinding fear. In those days, sexual harassment was not something you talked about to anyone.

One unbearably hot summer night I was resting in my attic room which had no ventilation and no insulation. I heard the switch in the attic hallway click. The thread of light beneath my door let me know I was in danger. I forgot about being hot and tired. Faith or no faith, I was scared to death.

The dead-of-night thoughts of what could happen made me drop quietly to my knees. I thought of Daniel in the lion's den and I prayed to his God. If God could provide Papa, the Kochs, and the Nielsons when I needed them, then surely he could send his angels to me now.

As I knelt by my bed I was frozen in fear. My heart was in my throat and fear overwhelmed me.

He pounded and pounded and kicked at the door. I knew he could easily break it down. Then I heard his brother joining him.

A miracle, God. I need a miracle, I prayed silently. Just then the phone rang and my would-be assailant went to answer it. Before he hung up I heard the lady of the house come home and I knew I was safe for the rest of that night.

I prayed desperately for a different job—one where my faith and call would be safe. The same peace I had experienced the night in the old Askov church overwhelmed me. I went to sleep knowing for certain that in the morning God would have an answer for me.

Today I thank God for those days when I lived in such danger. Throughout my ministry I have worked with abused children. I have taught them that when someone says, "If you loved me, you would," they need to reply, "If you loved me you wouldn't even be asking." Next to loving God, marriage is the most wonderful relationship on earth. Someone ought to be teaching our youth how to make it work. Too many young people settle for a cafeteria marriage. They take the first thing in line that looks good and pay for it at the end.

The next morning I saw another job advertised in the paper. It was maid's day off so with fear and trembling I went to apply.

I had one good dress, carefully ironed, and one pair of shoes, carefully shined. Papa had taught me that if you have a dollar and need a dress or a meal, take the dress. If you look right you might get a job which will take care of the meal. When I arrived at the house, the porch was filled with applicants, many much older, better dressed, more experienced, and surely better prospects for the job. But I knew something they did not know. I was God's missionary and if he wanted me to be a missionary, he would have to find a way for me to go to high school. My faith faltered a bit, however, as I wondered if they would choose someone who could work full-time.

I prayed God would let me answer the questions correctly and in some way share my faith. When it came my time for an interview, the woman of the house candidly asked me why she should hire me rather than some of the older applicants.

Come through for me, God! I prayed. Standing straight and tall I told her I thought that nobody ever does his very best. That is why each of us has a chance of doing better. That is exactly what I would do if hired. When it looked like I would be hired I told her I knew what I wanted to do with my life and that I would need a high school education to get it done.

Mrs. O'Mallory said their family was devoutly Catholic, that her husband was owner and proprietor of O'Mallory's department store and that she liked young people who knew where they were going. She asked about my call at great length.

I knew very little about Catholics except that in Milltown, where everyone was either Lutheran or Baptist, there was a scandal when a Baptist girl defied her parents and married a Catholic. I was frightened. If I told her I was going to be a missionary, perhaps she would feel I was a heretic, just as some of the children from other churches had been taught that Catholics were heretics. If that's what she thought, she might not want a Protestant taking care of her children.

Yet Papa had told me that faith is not faith unless it leads to action. With fear and trembling I told her what God had done for me and how I had to answer his call. I said I would get up very early in the morning before I went to school and work until all the work was done at night. Afterwards I felt a strange peace at having witnessed to my faith.

When I finished I saw tears in her eyes. Then she smiled and I saw laughter in her eyes and a kindness I shall always try to replicate.

"It's a good idea to take an interest in your future since that's where you will spend the rest of your life," she told me. "My husband once felt called to the priesthood. Somehow he was afraid to trust the future to God and in a moment of doubt he lost his dream. I wonder what his life would have been if he had answered God's call. His great wish now is that our eldest, Tommy, will become a priest."

God is good. I was glad I had been honest.

"When can you begin?" she asked me.

"Today!"

She said the salary was a whole $1.50 a week. Not only could I go to school, but the school was just down the street and I would not need street car fare to get there. With all that money I could make clothes for high school in the fall. God was teaching me so many lessons. I learned that if you witness to God, he also witnesses through you and takes care of your needs. As it turned out, Mrs. O'Mallory usually gave her used clothes to charity, and I guess she thought I was a worthy one. With a tuck here and a hem put up there, I went to school that fall in clothes that had come from O'Mallory's department store. I felt like a queen.

By supper time I was installed in a tiny maid's room at the end of a back staircase. It had a bed and a table and some hooks for clothes. I felt snug as a bug in a rug in this shelter in the time of storm.

Mr. O'Mallory was in his late forties with a pudgy shape like a teenager, as if no physique had intervened between boyish fat and middle-aged spread. His thinning grey hair, his eyes bright and usually red, the flush of his cheeks and his pocked round nose told me his vices. He was a heavy drinker but one who gallantly rose with true repentance at every confession.

He was president of the parish council and on Sundays counted the money from both the masses. Mr. O'Mallory was a pillar of the community. His store was next to Mr. Shauntecy's Bar and Grill. Often when Mrs. O'Mallory would send me down to the mercantile for some errand they would tell me that Mr. O'Mallory was "next door."

He took a great liking to me in a fatherly sort of way, and was intrigued that I wanted to be a missionary. I soon learned that he hoped I would instill a call to the priesthood in his oldest son Tommy.

One day when the O'Mallory baby fell against the heating stove I was dispensed to fetch his father at once. When he was not at the store I went next door. Mr. O'Mallory was rip-roaring drunk. When I told him about the baby's burn, he buried his face on the bar and started weeping.

"I'm a wretch, a drunken, sodden wretch. I've failed my family. I'm so drunk I can't even help Mrs. O'Mallory with the baby. If it dies I killed it. I was supposed to be a priest and now because I am a drunk, Tommy will never become a priest. Promise me, Rose, that you will talk to Tommy and tell him God wants him to be a priest."

"You are not a drunk and your baby is not going to die," I ventured. "You are one of the kindest men I have ever met and Tommy loves you dearly."

"Help him to be a priest and I'll never drink again," O'Mallory pledged. "Faith and begory, I'll never touch a drop again in my life." His eyes were pinched shut and his fat hands held an empty glass. He almost looked angelic in his pleading.

"Is that a promise?" I whispered, trying to coax him into sobriety.

"A pledge to the Almighty," he vowed. "I promised God once I would be a priest. But then I met Mrs. O'Mallory. She was so beautiful and I wanted her so much. I never loved anything so much as that little colleen. All the boys wanted her but I had to have her.

"It nearly killed me darling Mother when I got married. Now I have got to pay her and God back by sending Tommy to the seminary to be a priest.

Just get Tommy to be a priest and my lips will
never again touch the stuff."

"I'll do what I can, but you have got to stop
drinking," I said in desperation.

Mr. O'Mallory tried to smile. The sharp smell
of beer and liquor drifted from him. I got him to
his feet. His breath smelled like the bottom of a
bird cage. I asked the bartender for some strong
black coffee. We poured it down him and the bartender slapped his face and splashed cold water
on it.

We got him home and O'Mallory was stone sober for days. Mr. Shauntecy saw me on the street
and asked about him. "I promise you sobriety will
kill him. Better drunk than dead!" he predicted.

Well, I had also taken a pledge and it nearly
killed me. I soon found out that Tommy was
mighty glad to spend time with me and he didn't
care a hoot about my pledge to his father.

He had never been allowed to hang around the
maid but now his father gladly sent him out to the
kitchen to help me dry dishes. I tried to talk to him
about God. I didn't know if God wanted to call him
to the priesthood but I knew that if he did, Tommy
had better be a Christian before he tried to be a
priest. Pastor Nielson said a black man had told
him when he entered the ministry, "Remember,
you can't no more give somebody something you
ain't got than you can come back from some place
you ain't been."

Yes, Tommy would indeed have to be a Christian first. After all, too many men were just making a living from religion. So with all the zeal of a

Trappist monk I prayed and worked on Tommy. Tommy didn't seem to mind; in fact he liked being around me, but for all the reasons boys have always like girls.

Next Mr. O'Mallory decided I should help Tommy with his homework. I soon found out that his interest was neither in the priesthood nor his studies as much as in me. When he asked me to be his date for the school dance I knew I had flubbed my mission miserably.

Tommy was captain of the baseball team and the most popular boy at school. I was only his mother's maid. I should have been honored and I was not a little flattered. But I felt like a phoney. I had made an impossible pledge to his father who had been miserably sober for a whole long month. I knew that if Tommy were going to be a priest he could not be interested in girls. I also knew that if I were going to be a missionary I could not be interested in a boy who did not share my calling.

I wanted to talk to Papa but he was busy trying to keep things going at home. I had a job and was working. He did not need more problems.

I got up early and did the downstairs cleaning every day before I went to school. In the afternoon I hurried home and was finished with my work by eight. This left little time for me to study and I was expected to spend time with Tommy and his homework. My grades were slipping. I was finding myself burning the midnight oil to keep up with my studies.

One Friday night when I was serving fish Mr. O'Mallory did not come home. Mrs. O'Mallory sat stone faced through supper. She told the children their father was working late and then dispensed me to the mercantile to find her husband. She and I both knew the store had long since closed but she could not come to grips with the fact that he might be at Shauntecy's Bar.

Without ever admitting it to myself I had been wishing Mr. O'Mallory would get drunk just once to set me free from my promise. I should have been praying for his abstinence, for his eternal soul. Mr. Shauntecy had once told me that in the end drink would kill him and now I almost wished it had. I was ashamed to be thinking such thoughts. I just couldn't talk freely to Mr. O'Mallory about his faith because I badly needed this job and I just couldn't risk offending him by asking him if he were a Christian. After all, he was on the church council and a confidant to Father O'Leary and he was sure that would get him into heaven. He went to church twice on Sunday and to confession every time he fell off the wagon.

The whole thing didn't make sense to me. What was the purpose of any church, Protestant or Catholic, if they didn't know they were dealing with eternal life—heaven or hell?

As I approached Shauntecy's, Mr. O'Mallory fell out of the bar. He could hardly stand and his powerful breath was overwhelming.

All of a sudden I felt like a perfect failure. No wonder I couldn't witness to him. I had lied to him. I had told him I would try to get Tommy to be a priest when I knew good and well only God could call him. If God didn't call Tommy, neither could

I. Who was I to play God? I had just wanted to stop the drinking so badly and I had wanted to keep my job.

Now Mr. O'Mallory was trying to get on his feet. As he stood up I faced him squarely. He was bawling like a baby.

"I tried," he bellowed. The neon lights from the bar flickered in his face. He seemed like a stranger, all puffy and smelling so badly.

"I tried, too, but I failed you," I said in remorse. Job or no job I had to tell him that. I had to be released from my promise.

"You didn't fail me, Rose. It's all my fault!" O'Mallory blurted out.

"Your fault? No, it's my fault," I said. "I promised to do something I had no business promising you. I bribed you with a lie to keep you from drinking. Only God can call Tommy to the priesthood. I can't and never could. I should never have promised."

"No, no, you're not responsible for me. I'm a drunken failure. I've been a failure for years."

"No, you are not. You are a very good man and a good father and Tommy loves you. He has told me so many times. He's sorry to disappoint you and he thinks you are drinking because he won't be a priest. But he just can't be called to be a priest because you want him to or because you didn't become one. I am called to be a missionary. I can't ever be uncalled. I would be miserable being anything else. Tommy is just not called. Face it! He wants to be a doctor, a good Catholic doctor who will serve God with all his heart. He would be a miserable priest. Besides, I know he likes girls and it wouldn't work."

Mr. O'Mallory seemed to be sobering up. "I suspected as much. He told me once he loved you and some day wanted to marry someone just like you."

"I'm not good enough for Tommy. I'm just your maid and besides Tommy has lots of schooling ahead and I've got just as much. Neither Tommy nor I are going to make a mistake and think about getting married when God has years of education ahead for both of us. Besides, Tommy has red hair and doesn't look exactly like God."

Mr. O'Mallory was still too drunk to question that dumb remark.

"Tommy said I was a good man? That he loved me? He's a kind boy, a really kind boy. I promise I'll quit drinking."

"Tell you what," I said. "You do what you want to do. You can't quit for me or Tommy or Mrs. O'Mallory. Only giving your life to Jesus Christ can make you quit. He died for all your sins. Next time you go to church, just kneel down by that altar and ask him to be your Savior. The Bible says, 'He that believes on Jesus HAS eternal life.' If anyone truly accepts him he has power to become a new creature. That is the only thing that will stop you from drinking. Now, I won't bother you again if you will release me from my promise."

Mr. O'Mallory said he released me from my ridiculous promise and I started running home. I never turned to look if he went back to Shauntecy's. Mrs. O'Mallory had hinted that one day it would kill him. She was right. Two weeks later Mr. O'Mallory was dead.

It was time for me to get another job. He had drunk away most of the department store's assets and with the bills piled high Mrs. O'Mallory was talking of getting a job as a maid herself.

That would not be a simple task. Four million people were unemployed and the average wage was twenty cents an hour. Six thousand people lived in migrant camps in California. John Steinbeck wrote *The Grapes of Wrath*. Hundreds lived on the streets or died of starvation. Young men were anxious to be drafted, but a fourth of them failed the physical. Nutrition had been scarce during the depression. I knew I would need an education to be a missionary—I still needed to finish my senior year of high school—but how would I get the money?

I had learned a great deal during the years I spent with the O'Mallorys. Mrs. O'Mallory recommended me to a friend of hers who needed a maid and I took the job. Unfortunately, the friend lived five miles from school and could pay only one dollar a week. Ten tokens on the street car cost a dollar but I walked the five miles to school in the morning so I could save fifty cents a week for pencils, paper, and clothes. After school I had to take the streetcar so I could get home in time to work five hours before doing my homework and going to bed.

My grades slipped and I was frightened that I was not smart enough to get into Bible school or go to the mission field. (If I had only known that one day I would earn a doctorate and graduate with honors at age 50). Our failing school systems are emphasizing self-esteem, but I wonder if self-esteem does not also come largely from succeeding in academics. Mine slipped with my grades.

Those were very lonely days. My only contact with the church was through a woman named Mrs. Ericson. On Thursday afternoon, maid's day out, she prepared a free meal at the church so all the maids would have a place of fellowship. A prayer meeting always followed.

I was desperately lonely.

Chapter Fourteen

❄

"Miles to Go Before I Sleep"

*P*apa had worked and saved enough so Mama and the younger children could get a house in town. I sensed that things were not much different at home but I saw how hard Papa was trying to make things first class for Mama. I was far from Papa and seldom saw him; he had his hands full. I had a family but I was on the outside of it.

My new schedule left no time for making friends. I felt nobody but God cared where I was and often he seemed far away. I tried to share my faith but there was so little time. I didn't realize then that this experience was teaching me many things I would need to know when I became a clergy wife: how to entertain in style, how to make a house attractive, how to cook and serve meals, wash and iron, how educated people lived and dressed. I had time to think through a value system that would keep me from ever denying my call in order to pursue wealth. I discovered that money could buy a fine dog, but only love could make him wag his tail. The Nielsons and the Kochs had no money and yet they were far happier than those for whom I worked. Unhappiness is not having too little, I decided; it is wanting too much. "He is no fool who gives up what he cannot keep to gain that which he can never lose," a martyred missionary would later write.

I had a wonderful English teacher who introduced me to great literature and poetry. I loved Robert Frost and his poems "The Road Not Taken" and "Stopping by Woods on a Snowy Evening." I was grateful for those who had stood at the crossroads of my life to point me in the right direction. Now I had "promises to keep and miles to go before I sleep."

That year the winter's fury peaked just as final exam time came. I had to pass and I could not miss school so I set out one January morning when the radio said the temperature was 24 below zero with an even colder wind chill factor.

If I took the short cut through the enormous cemetery I could shorten the five-mile hike by one mile. The blinding, roaring winter storm provided only ten feet of visibility but I knew the tombstones well. I had walked there in the gold and yellow autumn when they had seemed like friendly allies, folks who had fought life's battles and left me a heritage. Now, with the blinding blizzard forcing me into a hunchback position, my eyelids freezing shut and my fingers and toes numb, each tombstone seemed like an enemy to be conquered.

The north sky was the color of burned-out campfire ashes. One more step, one more tombstone, one more dividing path. Now the monuments portended death, throwing a pall of helplessness over me as I fought the last mile. The tempest beat relentlessly and ignored all but me. It was me all alone, not another soul for miles, me and the storm. I felt as if I could not reach God. I was too numb to think, much less to pray. I seemed frozen into immobility, lost in the numbness of nothingness.

Suddenly I didn't care—not about graduating, the call or fighting any more. I wanted to sleep, to forget, to rest just a bit before I plowed on. The snow seemed like a warm blanket. What I wanted was warmth and a real live Papa and Mama who didn't abandon me to a graveyard to die.

Then in my confused mind I remembered the winter Papa almost died trying to reach the cattle. He had said, "Frostbite is nature's way of preserving heat by shutting down circulation to an extremity. Keep walking. Don't ever give up." Dimly, in some far distant wind, I heard Papa calling to me, saying those words again. It seemed he was walking toward me through the howling storm, through the merciless cold, and his hand was reaching out to me. *Keep walking, don't give up! Yes, Papa! Keep Walking!*

I inched my way toward him. Maybe he would die in the storm, too. I had to reach him so I kept going until I lost the image of him in the vision of

the school building. I thought I was reaching out
to grasp Papa's hand but it was the knob of the
schoolhouse door. Then I remembered no more.

I woke later that afternoon. My English teacher
was beside me. She told me my body had been
white, cold, and hard before it became red and
swollen. They had given me something to make me
sleep but now nothing could dull the pain. They
wanted to call my mother but I knew it best to
change that subject. I didn't want them to call my
boss because I might lose my job if she thought I
couldn't work. They talked of gangrene setting in.
I longed for Papa.

I did get permission from my boss to go home
with my teacher. All night she immersed my feet
and arms in warm water and then cuddled me in
cozy blankets and fed me warm liquids. I felt list-
less, drowsy, and confused. As the pain subsided
I fell asleep. When I awoke I learned that she had
arranged for me to clean the tables in the school
lunchroom. This job paid a whole $1.50 a week
plus a daily hot lunch. Now I would have car fare
so I would not have to walk to school in the mornings.

The skin which had been white and hard
turned red and blistered. Some of it turned black.
But I missed only one day of work. Actually, I was
glad for the pain. Without it I would not have had
money enough for a cap and gown. I had been sure
God and I would earn the diploma but I had not
thought I could afford to march in the procession
like a real graduate. Mama and Papa and all my
family would be there and I would prove I was first

class after all. The rest of the semester I lived for the monumental night when I would march across the stage and receive my diploma wearing a mortarboard.

On the Baltic coastline stands the chief port of modern Poland, Gdansk. The month I put on that noble cap and gown and grasped my diploma, Hitler invaded Poland on a broad front. The war for Danzig eventually engulfed the whole world and brought the death of fifty million people.

America should have taken heed, but for an America weary of the depression, World War II came along at a perfect time. The government shifted into high gear. Young men were enlisted full speed to train to fight the enemy. In Washington the government took complete control of nearly every aspect of life in America. Extraordinary powers were granted the government, not just to forbid the consumption of butter and sugar but to imprison Japanese-Americans who had committed no crime.

I dressed for commencement and waited for my family to come. I marched in the procession but I hardly remember it. I was too busy scanning the audience for my family.

The speaker expounded about changing the world. He said it is never changed by accident but that change is always the result of a deep faith, high intention, and daring to share a vision. The trailblazers of faith who are the world changers do not follow where the easy paths lead—they go where there is no path. It is the risk takers who will change the world. The poorest man is not the one without wealth but the one who has no call or vision.

I have often thought about that speech. The speaker was right. He said that each of us is a risk taker, a caretaker, or an undertaker. Caretakers are folks who simply take what another generation has left for them and use it without leaving anything better for those who follow.

Undertakers are bent on destruction. They take the melody out of music, the beauty out of art, the pride out of appearance, the romance out of love, the commitment out of marriage, the responsibility out of parenthood, the togetherness out of family, the learning out of education, the loyalty out of Americanism, God out of our schools, service out of patriotism, civility out of behavior, refinement out of language, dedication out of employment, prudence out of spending, ambition out of achievement, patience and tolerance out of relationships.

Undertakers are those who want to bury our world with hate and war, low vision and lack of dreams—like Hitler and Mussolini. Every generation is just one step from extinction, the speaker said. *Why, there are even undertaker preachers who kill churches,* I was thinking.

It is easy to avoid becoming a risk taker. All that is needed to make our entire world godless is one generation of young people who know nothing about God and one generation of adults who do not care. Would Hitler win? Would we have a godless world?

"We must take life by the tail and give it all we've got," the speaker continued. We can all be winners because winners are simply those who may have been counted out several times but didn't hear the referee. The credit belongs to the man or woman who is actually in the arena, whose face is marred by dust and sweat and blood and tears, who knows that the quality of life is in direct proportion to excellence in turning a hurting world back to God.

His speech was excellent and I was ashamed I was listening with only one ear. Where were Mama and Papa? He ended by saying that sometimes when we follow Jesus we have to learn how to look good on wood. These were the days when you could still talk about God, Christ and his message in the schools. We were all given a printed copy of the speaker's message. I think most of the students kept it. We would need it in the bitter days ahead. Many of the men and a few of the women who sat there that night, listening to the speaker assure them that the world is filled with opportunities, would die on the battlefields.

I read my copy of that speech often after graduation, almost memorizing it. But that night my mind was keenly on my family. They still had not come.

Then I saw Papa come in—alone. He had tried to get Mama to come and that was why he was late. I had been so afraid no one would come. Then, when I saw Papa walk in I realized he was plenty enough. He had always been plenty enough. He and God. I felt a huge lump in my throat and bit my lip to stop the tears. Life seemed too fleeting. I knew that never again would I be graduating

from high school like this. Never again would our
class be all together. The graduation march was
a prelude to marching off to war! Just as our family was not all together tonight, so the world was
divided. It seemed pure nonsense to be preparing
for war. Why couldn't we live together on this plentiful globe in peace and harmony?

I pledged to God I would always try to make
him and Mama and Papa proud of me. Some day
I would graduate again—and next time they would
surely all be there. I had wanted them all there
so much that night, to just once know I was first
class. I had hung in there when the lonely sled-
ding was all uphill. I had done it for them all, but
only Papa cared enough to come. Still, if I hadn't
wanted to make them proud, I would have dropped
out long ago and then God and I would be the
loser. It was a good lesson to learn. You serve God
and do his bidding no matter who cares.

There was no money for graduation presents,
but Papa gave me the finest gifts, which money
could not buy. After the ceremony he bought two
nickel sodas and we sat on a park bench to talk.
Across the traffic I could see the lights going out
one by one in my old alma mater, West High
School. I was filled with a bittersweet nostalgia
but not regret. That chapter was closed and the
greatest joy was that I had survived and won. It
was time to move on.

We sat for a long time just being glad we were
together. We were as close as we had ever been
and I felt so blessed. I had a family. I had Papa! I
had graduated. I had heard the call of God for my

life. Between us Papa and I had a millionaire's share of good memories. It takes time and love to come to that place and Papa and I had found that place with each other. He had his big arm around me. I felt so rich and blessed and happy.

The moon was rising great and golden. In the still, starry night fluffy clouds were floating gently like angel wings across the sky. The single sound was the street car clackety-clacking in the distance. A few stragglers came hurrying with their heads down, intent on getting home.

It would soon be time for Papa to go. I wanted to use the time wisely because soon I would have my loneliness all to myself and Papa would have his loneliness.

It was Papa who broke the spell. He told me how proud he was that I had graduated and that I belonged to the family of God . . . and how sure he was that he belonged to God. He said he was sorry that life had not been filled with all he had wanted for me. I could not believe that he could feel any regret for what life had brought to me. Every experience was the perfect preparation for my call. Every step of the way God had led us. Now finally tonight God had done a miracle and let me march with the others. I had been able to wear the mortar board and the long black robe. I was one step closer to being a missionary.

Hundreds of young people had not had that opportunity. Some of the young men who graduated tonight were looking forward to being drafted. Starting military salary was a whole $50 a month. Why, with all that money they could help support their families back home. For a fleeting moment I thought of the irony. Fifty dollars a month is not enough for which to die. But then that seemed a foolish thought. These boys were enlisting for a principle, for a Christian land with freedom to worship God. This is the land Papa and Mama had crossed an ocean and left everything to claim.

I did not have time to say good-bye to my classmates after graduation. Now I would never have that chance. Many of them would die on foreign soil. War seemed so senseless. Someone asked Abraham Lincoln about wars and he said, "The whole world fighting is just like my two sons crying. I have three walnuts and each boy wants two." Families and churches are no different. My emotions were quickly running the gamut.

That graduation night Papa talked to me as if it might be the last time we could share like this. The traffic had died down. A few night doves hooted softy and the tower clock chimed ten. He told me that never before had America been in such danger. Japan was arming for war with the scrap metal our country had sent there. Roosevelt had just sent seven million dollars in aid to England, an ally that was predicted to fall into Hitler's hands. There were blackouts and brownouts and America could be bombed. In Papa's beloved Denmark his brothers and sisters were living right next door to Nazi Germany and could be the next victims. It seemed like his old optimism was wearing thin.

"Oh, Papa," I said. "You gave me the church. You gave me a dream. You and I laughed and cried together and found Jesus together. You taught me to flee from discord when we could not solve it. You showed me that happiness is an inside job and that nobody can make us unhappy unless we give them permission." I thought of George Goethals who had built the Panama Canal despite harsh criticism. When asked how he would answer his critics he replied, "With the canal." Life had been good! I had answered our critics with a diploma.

Then Papa reminded me that stopping at third base adds no more to the score than striking out. I would need more education. But how? I knew that every cent Papa earned was needed at home.

As I clutched my diploma, a tiny sheet of white paper rolled up and tied with a gold ribbon, we talked about my call. He suggested that Northwestern Bible School in Minneapolis would be a good place to prepare for missionary service. Papa and Mama had found a way to send my second oldest sister there. She was determined to go to the mission field, too, and was training to be a nurse.

My favorite oldest sister had not gotten that help and had fled into a bad marriage. Papa felt remorseful about that. She had worked side by side with him in the fields and loved him as much as I did. He felt he should have tried to find a way for her to go to school. My gifted brothers had dropped out after grade school and were out working. Papa had been thinking long and hard about how to be certain that didn't happen to me.

"Do you remember when times were really tough and Mama would say, 'We'll all end up over the hill in the poorhouse'?"

I had heard it many times. Whenever Mama said that, I would conjure up a vision of the poorhouse. It kept me from ever thinking we were poor. Papa had always said that not having anything was no disgrace. It was only inconvenient. Poverty in itself is not dishonorable unless it comes from idleness, intemperance, extravagance, or folly.

No, I had never felt poor because I had never even been close to going to the poorhouse. The Kochs, the Nielsons, and Papa had seen to that. Poor people were all the folks who had come to the parsonage doors of my childhood. They came hungry and homeless and went away with much more than food.

Papa said, "How would you like to go to the poorhouse?"

I thought he was kidding and I began to laugh. But he wasn't joking.

"Man kan hvad man vil, men slid maa det til (You can do what you will, if you use all your skill)," he said softly under his breath. Whenever Papa said that I knew he had some grand scheme and I was all ears.

Papa explained that while working on a job he had met old Miss Miller. She had taught country school to three generations of young students, but she had just moved to the poor farm. Papa had taken her there. It seemed incredible. Her story was legendary. It had been written up in the *Progressive Farm* newspaper and she had even been interviewed by the radio station.

During all those years of teaching her meager salary had been spent giving away shoes, pencils, and paper to needy students and providing care for her ailing parents. When their farm was foreclosed and the old folks died of broken dreams she discovered she had more liabilities than assets.

Being proud and spunky, when people offered to take her in or provide for her keep, she replied, "There are God's poor and the Devil's poor." Jesus died God's poor, Luther died God's poor, Wesley died God's poor. They all died blessing the world. She said that if she had no money, God was calling her to the poorhouse and she'd find a way to go there as God's poor. She'd earn her keep.

She had been a teacher all her life and the poorhouse wouldn't change that. Since poverty of purpose is worse than poverty of purse, she guessed she was rich. Poverty even had some advantages. If you were poor it seemed the doctor would cure you faster. Poverty sticks with you even after most of your friends leave. Everyone wanted to take up a collection for her but she wouldn't hear of it.

She had always helped those most in need and she had found them again. Papa loaded up her few furnishings on his old pickup and took her over the hill. He was amazed at who was there, but Miss Miller wasn't! They were neighbors—sturdy, proud pioneers who had lost their health or their possessions in the depression, those whose bodies had been broken by hard work and malnutrition, those who had just run out of cope. Many were immigrants who had come to the land of golden opportunity and had with great reluctance checked in their pride at the door of the poorhouse.

Bumping along the country road, Papa had told Miss Miller all about me and my call. Miss Miller had solved too many dilemmas to let this one baffle her. Before they had unloaded her belongings she had the administrator of the poorhouse, a former student of hers, listening to my experiences as a maid, my dream of further education, my need for funds.

Experience is one thing you can't get on the easy payment plan. Yes, there was a job opening at the poorhouse. The salary was an unbelievable $25 a month and room and board. Recommendation and reputation—hers and Papa's—cinched the job for me. I could start in two days.

I was overwhelmed. Why, $25 a month was nearly what Rev. Koch had been paid to support his whole family the years I lived there. The minutes of the church board meeting had read, "Four hundred dollars a year and 20 cords of stove wood, ten of hard maple and ten of mixed hardwood."

The minister who followed him had gotten the same salary but I guess they had learned from Papa that a preacher needs a cow, so they had thrown in a milk cow to boot. Rev. Koch had returned Papa's cow when he left West Denmark. When Bess returned home she had fought all the other milk cows to get to her old stall. Papa had laughed and said the cow had learned a lot from being a church cow. He'd seen parishioners fight just as hard for their private pew.

As I sat on that park bench with Papa that night, my heart sang for joy. I had graduated from high school and had a good paying job! How could

I have doubted a God who had walked with me every step of the way? I would work this year and save for school next year. Little did I know how Northwestern Bible School would change my entire life!

Chapter Fifteen

Don't Go, Papa!

"Well, Papa, I am ending up over the hill at the poorhouse, rich as a king," I told him.

I began to laugh. Ideas were churning fast and furiously in my head. Every spare minute I would be at the poorhouse I would help Miss Miller. We could have crafts, plays, and music. A few women were beginning to work in defense plants and their children had no place to go after school. Why not drop them off at the poorhouse where grandmas and grandpas who needed to be needed could help the children with their homework? In my new job, I would be learning how to minister, how to help poor people, and how to build surrogate families for those who had none. I would do my best to win them all to Christ. *We could enlist churches to help,* I thought as my mind raced.

Then I turned to look at Papa. God had provided one miracle so now I asked for another for Papa. I hoped the next years would be kinder to him.

We sat there for an eternity without saying a word, and yet we each knew what the other was thinking. It's something you have to experience to truly understand.

My English teacher quoted a writer who said that sometimes a relationship surprises you and changes the way you look at the world forever. We all go through life touched in some way by relationships. If we are lucky, somewhere along the journey at least one relationship will change us for the better. Or at least change the way we look at things. Maybe it will motivate us. Or challenge us. Maybe it will move us in such a way that we will wonder, "Isn't this the way life is supposed to be?"

As I looked at Papa I wanted to stand up and shout, "This is the way it's supposed to be! Now why can't all relationships be this way forever?"

He had poured out his heart to me like I was an adult. Then I remembered that Papa and I had always shared that way. So many people had always seen me from the outside and never let me exist as my own person, an individual, worthy to be a part of the family. I was so proud and happy— until I realized Papa was working up to something. He didn't know how to start. It was like he had to say it but didn't want me to feel any pain. I was frightened.

Finally, he told me. The government was offering an unheard-of starting wage—eighty cents an hour—for men to sign up to work on the Alaskan Highway and to build military bases on the Aleutian Islands. But he would have to sign up for much too long. "The last years have been hard on Mama and the family," he explained. "Mama thought this would be a good idea."

I felt it was dead wrong. I felt deserted and desolate and I sensed he was feeling the same way. He told me about the day he became a naturalized citizen and said he was proud to be an American. He explained that America had been kind to him and this was a chance to help his country and Mama and the family. Only in America could I have graduated from high school with the chance to rise as high as I wished.

In just an hour it would be midnight. Then the last orange and black streetcar would come clackety-clacking down the street and this night would be history. We were both thinking the same thing and yet neither of us was saying it. *Papa,* my heart cried, *Please don't go so far away where the eternal wind blows across a frost-cemented, barren tundra.*

The golden moon had risen big and bright and I could see Papa clear as daylight. It was not the Papa I had known long ago. His hair was thin, his back was bent. The years had carved their autograph on his body. He was skin and bones. Food did not agree with him and his stomach always hurt. He needed fresh milk and vegetables. Who would see that he ate right? He was plagued with arthritis and often in pain. Who would keep him warm? I feared he would never come home alive. I knew those who love God never see each other for the last time. Death is not a period but a comma in the saga of life—but this comma was in the wrong place

My mind was racing with arguments against his going. He was desperately needed at home with his four small children who would never know the Papa I knew. It seemed such an extravagant waste. Surely he could find a job closer to home than Alaska. They were talking about building a defense plant at New Brighton—within driving distance from home.

Folks were saying that the depression was behind us. Prosperity was just around the corner . . . although few noticed that it was coming on the wings of war. On the coast, munition plants were humming with three shifts. Boeing was behind on orders for B-17s. Young men were leaving school and farms and shops to don Uncle Sam's uniforms in the greatest army the world had ever known. Why, oh why, go to the Aleutians? Jobs will soon be more plentiful here.

My heart was pounding so hard I was sure he could hear it.

"Papa you could work at home, make a little less and those at home could get to know how first class you are," I whispered. I couldn't get more words out. I knew that he had weighed all these arguments in his mind and it had made no difference. Why hurt him again? The world was turning on its axis, tomorrow the sun would rise, and

Papa would be gone. *Time, stop! World, stop turning! Let me think if this is right.*

Of all the sadness I had ever felt in my life, this was the greatest. What a shame it was that everybody in the world had not realized how first class Papa was. And now it was too late. All my life I had tried to be inside the family and so had Papa. We had not been able to control life. Like a great curse we would always be on the outside. And now he would be on the outside halfway around the world where I could never see him.

The school clock chimed midnight and the last orange and black nearly empty streetcar was clackety-clacking far away. We had only a few minutes left.

"Papa, don't leave. Please don't leave! I need you! We all need you so much." I didn't want to cry. I knew he thought he had to go and I wanted him to remember this as a night of joy.

"It is best," Papa said with resignation that must have sounded like Rosa's so long ago when she could not change their world. "There is wisdom in knowing what you cannot change."

We both knew what he meant. The streetcar was stopping and I had not stopped the world . . . or Papa from going. I wanted to give him something to take with him.

"Here, Papa, take this. You earned it. Keep it to remember me by," I said as I crushed my diploma into his hand and gave him a final hug. He swung onto the streetcar just as it was taking off.

He kept waving from the platform. He was just standing there waving my diploma until the night enveloped him and the streetcar clanked its way around the corner. The last I glimpsed of him he seemed to be standing in the cold darkness of the northern lights and the barren tundra.

I could not sleep that night. I had wanted to give him so much more. I had wanted to explain to everyone what they were missing—what genuine first class was really all about!

The next day I packed everything I owned into two cardboard boxes, took the streetcar to the bus station and the bus to the Ramsey County Poorhouse. Except for Papa being so far away, it was the happiest year of my life up to that point. Miss Miller took me under her wing and taught me how to study, to fix my hair, and to sew clothes for college. I no longer felt like an ugly duckling. More than that, she taught me how to translate my faith into deeds. It gave me self-confidence. The poor, the old, the lonely, the forgotten were won to Christ. I made wonderful friends and heard great stories of covered wagons, sod houses, and courage which was surely misplaced in the poorhouse. I tried to forget that Papa was halfway around the world every time I opened my heart to someone else's Papa.

Miss Miller provided a college year's worth of horse sense and knowledge. Her fascinating tales of her teaching experiences confirmed in my heart Rev. Koch's hunch about my ability to teach. When I later became a teacher, Miss Miller was my role model.

I missed Papa terribly and prayed for him passionately. Our thoughts and prayers crossed the miles and we kept in touch with endless letters. Once he wrote that there was a beautiful woman behind every tree. Even in those harsh surroundings Papa was full of humor—there was not a single tree on the island.

The gale winds blew night and day. He worked seven long days a week and as much overtime as he could get. He sent money home and saved every cent he could in war bonds which he felt would assure that the four children at home would not have to struggle with high school and college as I had. Meanwhile, his two young sons were growing up without a single memory of him.

He wrote that Denmark seemed millions of years ago and that dreams were sometimes elusive. He ached for his children but never complained. He seldom wrote about the dark, ten-month winters when the sun came out only a short part of the day. Instead he painted the northern lights in such splendor that I felt we stood shoulder to shoulder watching their fireworks.

During the brief sunlit summers he wrote more frequently describing the exquisite beauty of the resplendent wildflowers that blanketed the tundra with a brilliant rainbow. Far from the farm life he had once known, he waited with joyous enthusiasm for the brief summertime when the wildlife made up for time squandered in hibernation by cavorting on the sunlit wasteland.

There was no chapel, no church, just Papa's faith, a few rough workmen, a few Aleuts, his Bible, and the perpetual howling wind day in and day out. But that didn't stop Papa from witnessing. Hardly a letter arrived that didn't tell of someone he had led to Christ. Small wonder that eventually all his children, his grandchildren, even down to his great-grandchildren and so many more that he met along the way became Christians. The thousand-mile chain of 20 volcanic, treeless, barren islands stretching out of the Alaskan peninsula was uninhabited save for a few small villages of native Aleuts scattered along the archipelago. It seemed to me like Papa's prison, but actually it was his mission field.

In one of his final letters to me he wrote, "Always consider yourself a first class citizen of God's kingdom. Jesus gave you that right when he died on the cross."

Papa was a peacemaker who despised conflict. Ironically, though, in trying to escape conflict he was building for war. There was talk that the Russians would invade the Aleutian Islands. They claimed they belonged to them anyway since they were certain they had broken off from Russia, not Alaska. As for me, in moments of missing Papa, I would have been glad to give the islands back to the Russians if it could bring Papa home.

Once when I ventured to ask Papa to come home he answered with an excerpt torn out of an Alaskan newspaper. It was Abraham Lincoln's response to his critics:

> I desire to conduct the affairs of my country so that if at the end, when I come to lay down my reins, I have lost every other friend on earth, I shall at least have one

friend inside me. I do the very best I can; and I mean to keep on doing it to the end. If the end brings me out all right, what is said against me will not amount to anything. If it brings me out all wrong, then a legion of angels swearing I was right will make no difference.

Papa sent a picture of himself beside a Quonset hut on the treeless expanse of nowhere. He looked bent and broken, yet I still saw in him the undaunted immigrant pioneer spirit. His hair was nearly as white as the driven snow on which he stood firmly and a bit forlornly planted. Furrows as clearly punctuated as those he had plowed on the recalcitrant prairie were carved deep in his face.

Although Papa never mentioned it in his letters, adding to my worries about Papa was the news that 2,600 Japanese soldiers had invaded two of the Aleutian Islands—Attu Island and Kiska Island. On May 11, 1943, one of the bloodiest battles of the war was fought at Dutch Harbor. July 26, 1943, brought the final battle in the Aleutians and the Japanese left defeated.

Oh, Papa, I prayed desperately, *Please come home—alive!*

I lived for Papa's letters and wrote back long cheery epistles. I asked about his food. The fresh milk, fruits, and vegetables he needed for his stomach ailment all came frozen, powdered, or dried and made him sick, so he ate little. He sent me a

poem by Grantland Rice called "Two Sides of War"
which I kept for years. It read:

> All wars are planned by old men in council
>   rooms apart,
> Who plan for greater armament and map
>   the battle chart.
> But out along the shattered fields where
>   golden dreams are gray,
> How very young their faces are where all
>   the dead men lay.
> Gray haired and solemn in their pride, the
>   elders cast their vote
> For this or that or something else, which
>   sounds the warlike note.
> But where the sightless eyes stare out,
>   beyond life's vanished joys
> We've noticed nearly all the dead are
>   merely girls and boys.

Chapter Sixteen

A Road Not Taken

*P*apa wrote that he was praying for me and I felt like his prayers were being answered. Sometimes it almost seemed like he was beside me, cheering me on.

With the year at the poorhouse over and money for tuition in hand, new clothes, new lessons learned and new determination to be a missionary, I set out for Northwestern, a four-year Christian college for missionaries in Minneapolis. It helped that I was busy learning to be a missionary because I had less time to miss Papa.

Mr. Bass taught personal soul winning at Northwestern. "By your fruit you will know them," he quoted scripture, adding, "Fruit is not just talk. It is winning." Nothing I would learn later equalled the vision and dreams he and the other

Northwestern professors planted in my heart. They constantly said, "You will never be great when you graduate unless you practice greatness now," and, "You must always walk your talk." I established habits which have lasted a lifetime. After all, when we get to heaven God is going to ask, "Whom did you bring with you?"

My experiences at Northwestern shaped my life so strongly that when I graduated from a denominational seminary many years later a professor stopped the graduation ceremony and announced, "The tragedy with this woman is that we didn't change her theology one whit." He was right. What I learned at Northwestern stayed with me through four more degrees. It worked and I wasn't about to fix it.

The man who made that comment during the graduation ceremony was the professor who began his class by asking us to list the myths in the Bible. I raised my hand and asked him to define a myth. He explained that a myth is a nice story like George Washington and the cherry tree that teaches a good moral but probably didn't happen. I spoke no more in that class. I needed the credit.

During that quarter, I watched students who entered the class with zeal leave it with nothing but doubts about what to preach. No wonder churches are empty. Folks have enough doubts without coming to church for more. People need to know what you know for sure! It seemed ludicrous that those who felt called to preach the gospel would disbelieve the only Book on which their call was based. I tried to tell them so.

On the last day of the class the professor was still concerned about the question I had asked on the first day. He said he had thought I was a housewife entering a second career and did not realize I was already a professor in a fine church-related university. He wanted to know how I could have a doctorate and still question that there were myths in the Bible. He spent the hour courting confrontation, but Papa had taught me better.

Finally, when the professor refused to dismiss the class without an answer I said, "Sir, it is true that I have a doctorate and teach psychology and counseling at a good Methodist college. However, after I have given students everything Jung, Freud, and Rogers theorized, I find that the real changes in behavior come only when they have accepted Christ and become new creatures in him.

"I have led many of my students to Christ," I continued prayerfully. "Their lives have been dramatically changed. Some have gotten off drugs and alcohol, others have found a new direction and purpose for their lives. Many of those who accepted Christ went to Viet Nam . . . several died there. Others have gone to distant mission fields, some to die there. One does not die for a myth."

After the class was over, knowing that I would probably receive a failing grade, I headed for the seminary president's office. Since by this time I had an earned doctorate I was not as threatened as I might have been earlier. I brought along my transcripts from Northwestern College and Northern Baptist Seminary. I had 120 hours of Bible, Greek, homiletics, and related studies which had

served me 30 years as pastor's wife and missionary. My husband and I had seen dead churches re-
vived, souls saved, and communities changed. Our
churches were consistently first in the state in pro-
fessions of faith.

I told the seminary president we had simply
done what Wesley had taught his ministers to do:
"Offer them Christ." I quoted Wesley's foolproof
recipe for church growth:

> You have nothing to do but win souls.
> You have nothing to do but be a missionary
>   church.
> You have nothing to do but live a holy life.
> Then you have nothing to do but rejoice.

The president of the seminary examined my
record in ministry. He saw that both my husband
and I had won national awards for church growth.
He scratched his head and leaned back in his
leather chair. Then he picked up the phone, called
the registrar and told him I had the credits to
graduate.

Pastor Nielson once said, "I don't mind being
a doormat for Jesus. I just don't want to write
'welcome' on it." This philosophy paid off that day.
I hope my action was a way of strengthening that
seminary for our denomination.

Fighting and criticizing never improve anything. Someone said that if you work for a man,
in heaven's name work for him! If he pays you
wages that supply your bread and butter, work for
him, stand by him and the institution he repre-
sents and try to leave it better than you found it.

By the time I enrolled at Northwestern, I was no longer a child wearing cast-off clothes. My freckles were gone. My red hair had turned a light auburn. I had saved enough to buy a new wardrobe. Until I accepted Christ I had not liked my name or my appearance. One day I read in the Bible about the Rose of Sharon. After that I embellished every signature with a tiny rose. I loved my name, I loved life, and I loved the golden door of opportunity God had placed before me.

It is a funny thing about life. If you refuse to see anything but the best you usually get it. I could not believe God had been so wonderful. I was no longer a child depending on Papa. I had grown into a young woman with a crystal-clear call of God upon her life. Wherever he wanted me to go, whatever he wanted me to do, I was his.

My grades in high school had not been the best. There had been too many long hours spent working before I could get to my studies. But now, even though I was working as a waitress, my grades were excellent. This seemed like a gift from God and gave me self-esteem. I had always known that the quality of one's life is in direct proportion to one's commitment to excellence every step along the way. Finally, I felt like I was on target.

I learned the Bible verse which we were required to learn each day and enrolled in personal evangelism classes and soul winning classes as did all my colleagues. I believed with all my heart that what you are going to be, you are becoming. I could not be a great soul winner on some faraway mission field if I were not a great soul winner now.

We developed an idiosyncrasy which some Christians never learn. We shared Christ on the streetcars, with the bakery clerk, with children we met. Amazingly, many were won to Christ by those of us who were short of everything but enthusiasm. I had been given some wonderful role models in the Nielsons, the Kochs, and Papa. They never missed a chance to live Christ both by word and by deed.

Everyone worked his way through school, yet each week we were given a specific assignment in a mission, church, or Sunday school. We were expected to be soul winners and prove ourselves before we graduated and went out to serve God.

Throughout life God has never given me cake without also giving me the frosting! It would have been wonderful enough simply to be in a school where everyone was confronted daily with God's call. Northwestern was connected with the great First Baptist church of Minneapolis. My high school days had been lean and I was starved for the feeling of love and warmth I had grown up with in the church. Wisely, Dr. Riley, the president and founder of our school, never locked the door of the sanctuary.

Morning after morning I would slip into that magnificent structure just as the stained glass windows shared the morning light that was breaking across the bustling city. There on my knees I found a new sweetness and joy in Jesus, and a new filling of his Holy Spirit to pour out to the lost. I wrote about this to Papa, who must have felt forgotten on the bleak, barren tundra. We figured out the time difference and tried to join each other in prayer. My waitress tips were often spent on a little package to send him, some warm mittens, boxes of cookies, love notes which only he and I would understand. I desperately prayed for his happiness and I poured out my thanksgiving to him for guiding me to this good school.

I also shared another confidence with him. I did not want to go to the mission field alone. I wanted to belong to someone as sweetly as the Kochs and the Nielsons had belonged to each other. Papa wrote back, "Seek ye first the kingdom of God and his righteousness and all these THINGS shall be added unto you." How wise he was.

It was easy to date at Northwestern. Students got to know each other well as they went out together on mission teams. We were told to choose our life's mate carefully for this one decision would determine 90 percent of our happiness or misery.

But I knew that much more than my happiness depended upon my choice of a mate. I had the call of God on my life and would have to marry someone who felt equally called. A successful marriage, I knew, depended on two things: finding the right person and then being the right person. I had seen marriages that were merely compromises—two people getting what neither of them wanted.

I did meet one young man, though, whom I shall call John, who was tall, dark, handsome, witty—and going to the mission field. I found myself being teamed with him over and over again. If I chose a practical work assignment, he always found a way to end up on my team.

I spent the summer before my senior year teaching Bible school in Montana. When I came home I did not have enough money to enroll so I worked until the middle of October in the new Brighton Defense Plant. How I wished Papa had stayed home and worked there. My wages were better than his!

The war effort was in full swing. "Remember Pearl Harbor" was the war cry. Two million Japanese people, most of them American citizens, had been herded into relocation camps, but nobody protested. California had three million new residents, all of whom had good jobs in war plants. Efficiency was making two new liberty ships a day. The ships of war were launched with champagne as lonesome sailors far from their wives and sweethearts sang "Harbor Lights," "The Green, Green Grass of Home," and "Pistol Packin' Mama, Lay that Pistol Down."

For six weeks I, who hated conflict, inspected thousands of bullets as they came by on the conveyor belt. War seemed like the ultimate family feud—you can't win it and you can't end it. I knew the real war to end all wars would not be fought with bullets.

Northwestern gave me permission to pick up my homework each day, but I was not allowed to move into the dormitory until after I had earned my tuition. By then, all my friends had roommates. The only room left was with a girl I knew nothing about. I reluctantly opened the door of the assigned room to meet one of the dearest, most precious friends I would ever make. She and I soon chose to do our required practical work assignment together.

I was not attached to anyone but when I did date John or someone else I thought it would be fun to have this roommate along. So I fixed her up with my brother who was working on a farm so we could double-date. Before the year was up they had found God's will for their lives. Looking back at all the couples God has let me help match, I know this has been one of the best. I not only found a wife for my brother—I found a true sister. God has made them a great soul-winning team as they have raised a wonderful family and worked at Bible camps. They even went to Africa to help build a mission hospital for my youngest brother, a great soul-winner who for 35 years has been a pilot with Missionary Aviation Fellowship. God had his eye on our family even when we could not see his guiding hand.

I was graduated at the end of three years and opted to attend the seminary for another year to get a Bachelor of Religious Education degree and to negotiate with mission boards. John was certain now that I was God's choice for him. I was not sure. When we broke up that spring his last words to me were, "If you ever change your mind, just write me a letter. I am going to be waiting for you."

During the Thanksgiving holiday that last year at the seminary, with Papa in the Aleutians and all the students home for vacation, I felt very lonely. I would be going away for language study in a year. The closer the time came to my going alone to some distant mission field, the more my faith was tested. I had seen students give up the holy call for marriage or money and had seen how miserable they became. They seemed to live their lives as an explanation instead of an exclamation. Nevertheless, I could understand how they were tempted to betray their call.

John kept writing to me, insisting I was God's choice for him. He had the right theology and plenty of charm, but I had a nagging doubt. He could preach like a pro and played a silver trumpet almost like the Angel Gabriel, so nobody seemed to notice what I noticed. John talked a good game but he had never led a soul to Christ. When I tried to picture myself on the mission field with him, something seemed wrong. Unless we knew the reason for going, how could we succeed?

Christmas was coming. I thought of spending Christmas without family and in a moment of weakness dropped a card to John who was attending seminary in the Dakotas. He answered by return mail. He would plan to be in Minneapolis for Christmas.

During the days ahead I had a nagging, sick feeling in the pit of my stomach. I wrote Papa and he wrote back on a simple post card: "Never marry until there is such a oneness between you that when one weeps the other will taste salt." He had not preached at me but I knew he was praying.

During these days of turmoil, Alf, a fellow student who had transferred from Northern Baptist Theological Seminary in Chicago, showed me a picture of his former roommate, Oscar Grindheim. Oscar was a young Norwegian who had come penniless to Northern Baptist Theological Seminary aboard the last boat to leave before the Nazis stormed his homeland.

Alf had been in Greek class with me and had mentioned Oscar several times before but I had paid little attention. This time, however, when Alf showed me the photo and told me he had invited Oscar to come to Minneapolis during semester break, I listened. As surely as God spoke to me at the altar long ago, I knew as I looked at that picture that a miracle was happening. Yes, Oscar was tall, dark, and handsome, with deep-set, purposeful eyes and an uncommon character in his face which could not be mistaken for synthetic piety. I sensed a depth of God's love which seemed to equal Rev. Koch's. A ridiculous peace, an uncanny calm and surety I had never known before encompassed me. The Holy Spirit had taken my concerns out of my bungling hands and into his nail-scarred ones.

I said nothing to Alf. I had no idea how God would work out the details but I knew they were in his hands. When Alf asked to borrow $20 of my tip money to buy Christmas presents for his wife and baby I did not know that he would actually use it to send Oscar a bus ticket. Alf sold encyclopedias to get through school and had often borrowed my tips when his sales were slim.

It was too late to get in touch with John who was driving in a blinding snowstorm in his $60 dilapidated depression era Ford across the icebound Dakotas. He arrived at Northwestern at midnight, slept in the car in near zero weather, and arrived at the dormitory nearly frozen to death the next morning. It was unthinkable that I had been playing games by inviting him to come. He was absolutely certain that now I would marry him.

I was ashamed and embarrassed. I knew it would be idiotic to tell him that God was to blame for my lack of faith, a faith I had tested at John's expense. I knew that was a lie.

I faced a moment of bitterest truth. For four years single missionary women had spoken in our chapel when they were home on furlough. I had talked to saints who had lived alone in distant, dangerous jungles for a lifetime in order to win natives to the Lord. When they finally retired their family and friends were all gone and they died as lonely as they had lived. I had always told God I would go anywhere, do anything, pay any price— but I had not been honest. I had not trusted him enough to go whether I was single or married.

God had led me step by step along a royal roadway. Now here at the final departure point for the mission field was I willing to trade God's perfect will for security? I should have known that I was happier in God's will than I could be anywhere else in the entire world outside of his perfect will. How could I have forgotten the lessons of my childhood?

Most students had gone home for the holidays so it was not hard to find a room for John. We talked. His arguments seemed sensible. He asked if I had met someone else. I had to tell him I had not, that I had no idea whether I ever would.

I could not tell him my inner struggle—that if God did not send Oscar then I must be totally committed to going out alone. Like Abraham as he placed Isaac on the altar, I had to be willing to make any sacrifice. Deep inside I guess I was hoping God had a ram in the thicket for me. But for the moment I had to leave all my life—my hopes and yearnings, my call to missions—on that burning altar and let God decide whether he would provide the ram.

I knew that if I sent John home I would lose him forever. I did not make the decision lightly. Our emotions were running high and John seemed to have all the facts. His mind was like concrete—thoroughly mixed and permanently set. He was going to the mission field. I was going to the mission field. He did not want to go alone or with anyone else but me. I had not met anyone else; I had only the dream.

John had not learned that when someone makes a mistake you rub it out, you don't rub it in. I thought of Papa's marriage. Papa had not been a Christian when he married. I wanted more for both of us. John's call was also at stake and he deserved more than what I could offer him.

I had written sparingly to Papa about John. I knew that if it were right, Papa would have to be the first to know. Why had I hesitated? I had no one to confide in now except Mother R., my dorm mother. We prayed together. She did not preach to me or presume to know God's will. She simply called me into her private apartment and showed me a treasured plaque I had seen hanging on her wall. She told me her husband had given it to her before they were married. It read, "Of all things, be of love the most careful."

John and I went to church together and he told them to put us in the young married folks' class. He beamed as he tried to show me what I was missing. It did look comfortable.

After church we went to a tiny restaurant for lunch. It was empty except for the lovely Japanese American family who owned it. They had been spared relocation but not discrimination.

John wanted to talk about nothing but my decision. He was going back to seminary that day. I silently begged God for a sign, a way to help this precious friend understand why we were not right for each other. I longed desperately to leave John better than I found him. He had enriched my life and loved me unconditionally. The pain was excruciating.

I'd asked God for a miracle and he was coming through again. The Japanese family, even though they were third-generation American citizens, were hurting deeply. Their restaurant was being boycotted because of animosity against the Japanese who were at war with us. God opened the door for me to gently share my testimony with them, the pain and the pleasure. John sat silently and was utterly amazed as all five accepted Christ. We shared hugs and love which had nothing to do with Pearl Harbor.

It was a bittersweet moment. John understood, as he listened to me lead them to Christ, why I could not marry him. The Japanese family knew another truth, that God's love transcends war and hatred.

We walked silently back to the dormitory. John picked up his bags. We would never see each other again. He hugged me tightly, turned his back and began to go. Then slowly he retraced his steps in an irrevocable, final farewell. Tears brimming in our eyes, he took both my hands in his. I saw a new spirit in him. I knew he understood why we were different, why it could not be.

"And to think it took the Japanese family to show us," he said. "Rose, you have blessed my life and set me in a new direction. I'm sad that I had to lose you to learn this, but my life will never be the same after that lesson in Japanese."

We both sensed a peace we had never felt between us before. I knew that God's Holy Spirit had his hand on him and would take care of both of us. I also knew that I had been sent into his life so that God could give him a new soul-winning missionary purpose.

When I went back to my dorm room I got on my knees to ask God's forgiveness for hurting John and for ever doubting my Savior. When I rose to face the new day I knew I had not made the decision because of Oscar. I had made it regardless of Oscar.

Chapter Seventeen

Valhalla

I worked double shifts during the rest of the school vacation to keep from thinking. I lived secure in the knowledge that God had me in his pocket. I knew nothing of the future except that my life was totally in his hands. God was in the driver's seat and would not let me make the same mistake twice. "He who dwells in the shelter of the Most High will rest in the shadow of the Almighty" (Psalm 91:1). What is faith but believing what you do not see? It was the closest I had ever walked with God. The Holy Spirit truly was hiding me in the cleft of the rock and teaching me that problems are often just opportunities for growth and self-mastery.

At the restaurant where I worked, customers were in the holiday spirit and tips were generous.

For many years I had not had the luxury of buying an entire new outfit. The stores were having after-Christmas sales and with a toss of my head I remembered Mrs. Nielson's "vel, of course." Perhaps it would be good therapy for a lost relationship. The outfit I bought was fire engine red with sparkling gold buttons. I splurged on bright red shoes for $1.99 and a stylish 99¢ haircut. It made me feel like a first class citizen again and covered a fresh wound which needed healing.

I spent a lot of time in the silent, cold sanctuary just letting God help me grow. I wrote Papa and he wrote back, "You made a wise choice. Just remember that sometimes when you marry your knight in shining armor you also have to be ready to clean up after his horse." I had taken that letter unopened to the church to savor in my loneliness. Now I laughed the familiar laugh Papa and I had shared so often.

The surprised custodian came in to ask if I were all right. Yes, I was all right. Papa had put me back on course. God was in charge of my life and I was in charge of my attitude and nobody was going to choose that for me. As I sat there I remembered Papa saying that marriage was a lifetime commitment, a covenant before God—not just a contract. You weren't married for better or worse, you were married for *good*. With God's help you stayed with it for life if you possibly could and tried your best to make it work. Papa's life had proven that. Even in marriage Papa had been a promise keeper! It had not always been easy. Nobody had worked at it more than Papa.

Students came back from their holiday break and finals were before me. I burned the midnight oil. I heard no more about Oscar even though Alf sat next to me in Greek class every day. I did not ask. I had little time to think of him anyway. I had to pass and I have never studied harder or had more demanded of me. The war was on and the school didn't want any draft dodgers.

Any man who failed in school had to report to the draft board. Many students would soon be leaving for India, Burma, Africa, South America, and the islands with little preparation beyond what they had gotten at that school. It had to plant us so firmly in God's word that neither death nor life, angels nor powers, things present nor things to come could separate us from the love of God that is in Christ Jesus (see Romans 8: 38-39).

When the finals were over at last I returned to my dorm room emotionally and physically tuckered out. I was dog-tired and had lost my voice. I was ready to take a steaming bath and spend an eternity in sleep.

I ran a tub of nearly boiling water and opened my Bible. As the delightful steam filled the chilly room, I read out loud to myself,

Praise our God, O peoples,
    let the sound of his praise be heard;
he has preserved our lives
    and kept our feet from slipping.
For you, O God, tested us;
    you refined us like silver.
. . . we went through fire and water,

but you brought us to a place of abundance.
May God be gracious to us and bless us,
    and make his face shine upon us;
may your ways be known on earth,
    your salvation among all nations.
(Psalms 66: 8-10, 12 and 67:1-2.)

I marked the date in the margin of my Bible:
January 31, 1944. I pulled down the shades and
relaxed long and luxuriously in the splendor of the
bath and a semester well done. As I washed my
hair and put it up and snuggled into my cozy pink
flannel nightgown, I wrapped myself in the warm
coverlet of God's love. I was ready to forget that
there was a world out there to win, exams to write,
or decisions to be made. A tiny snow sparrow sat
on my window ledge. As sleep enveloped me, I
prayed, *Lord, take over. I'm going to sleep.*

Then I heard the dormitory phone ring in some
faraway place. Mother R. was calling me from a
deep sleep. It was Alf. "Ruth and I would like you
to come to dinner tomorrow night. We have a
friend we want you to meet." I accepted his invitation, went back to my room and set the alarm
for tomorrow, glad that I had relegated this night
to God. *Keep your eye on me, God,* I prayed, *and
by morning I will be able to sort things out.*

I awoke to find that I had slept through the
night and the alarm clock and it was afternoon.
My voice was back and my brand-new, crisp fire
engine red linen suit with the sparkling gold buttons beckoned me from the closet. Adding a white
ruffled blouse, gold and red earrings and a touch

of makeup, I took a long look in the mirror. With a prayer in my heart, I was ready: *God, here I come.* But first I jotted a note to Papa:

> Dearest, dearest Papa, thank you for teaching me to follow a star, that love alone can transform the world, that marriage is an empty box that remains empty unless you put in more than you take out, that problems are opportunities in work clothes, that in the middle of every difficulty there lies an opportunity. How rich I am to have known you, Papa *Jeg elsker dig* (I love you). *Din egen lille Rosa* (Your own little Rosa).

Today I needed to think of Rosa and Papa and the ten years he worked and dreamt and then lost her. I wasn't sure why.

Leaving the dorm, I stepped into a winter wonderland. Softly to myself I quoted a poem my English teacher had us memorize:

> The snow had begun in the gloaming,
>   And busily all the night
> Had been heaping the fields and the highways
>   With a silence deep and white.
> Every pine, every fir, every hemlock,
>   Wore ermine too dear for an earl,
> And the poorest twig on an elm tree,
>   Was ridged inch deep with pearl.
> (from Longfellow's *First Snowfall.*)

The street lights wore diamond halos and the towering Norwegian pine wore ermine indeed. The snow underfoot crunched merrily as I strode with sure steps. Skaters were floating in graceful ease across the frozen lake. Children were throwing snowballs. I picked one up and tossed it to them. They laughed and tossed it back. I felt like a little girl again, on a mystical journey following the yellow brick road to God knows where.

Ruth and Alf made their home in a tiny one-room housekeeping apartment overlooking beautiful Loring Park. In summer they could watch swans and water lilies that were replaced in autumn by the flaming red and gold of Indian summer. But all the beauty of past seasons now was surpassed by an iridescent blanket of sparkling alabaster. Lovers walked arm in arm across the magnificent blanket of white. By the lake some children pushed an enormous oversized snowball, the dorsal of a gigantic snowman.

The brief day was waning, giving in to a great full moon that was bent on reflecting the winter gloaming. Stamping snow from my boots, I climbed the rickety stairs to the third-floor apartment.

Alf had heard me coming and because the baby was crying and Ruth was busy taking dinner from the oven, he had sent Oscar to open the door on the landing. My eyes were adjusting from the silvery white world and I did not see him. As I ran up the landing, light in heart, ready for whatever surprise God had in store for me, I ran smack dab into him.

I hadn't meant for it to happen like this. The slippery snow, still clinging to my boots, sent me careening to the floor. I was embarrassed until I laughed out loud thinking, *I didn't arrange this*

meeting and if God arranged for us to meet this
way, I must be hearing snickers from heaven. I began to laugh at the joy of being on an adventure
of utter abandonment to a God I trusted with every secret desire of my innermost being.

No more trying to figure things out like I had
with John. This time I would not pull a single
string or manage any convenient circumstances
which might end in another "Dear John" disaster.
Nope, this time I had left everything to God's
Spirit—well, almost. I *was* decked out in a red go-
to-meetin' outfit sporting a new hair do, red earrings, a perky red beret and a few drops from a
$5 bottle of Chanel No. 5 perfume.

In my secret heart did I think these things
might help me be first class? Maybe! But it hadn't
worked out that way and I began laughing. I
should have known. Hadn't I had been a fourth
class ugly duckling when God found Rev. Koch for
me? Wasn't I wearing a hand-me-down, mission
barrel, too-long, faded, dismally fourth class dress
on that blistering hot day when the good Samaritan named Pastor Nielson had stopped along the
roadside and bound my wounds?

I should have remembered by heart that God
had always stood at the crossroads and stair land-
ings of my life to do miracles a thousand times
more first class than I could do in my own
strength. I hoped I hadn't flunked the lesson he
had tried to teach me the day John drove off into
an eternal farewell. I'd begged God then, down on
my knees, to make me and my call his personal
property. In that miserable moment when I knew

I had failed God all I wanted was the wonderful privilege of knowing that he was in charge of his call on my life at last, forever and ever. Now God had written me a little reminder.

With Norwegian wit and a grin Oscar reached down to help me to my feet. We both laughed while I struggled to adjust my hat and rearrange my wounded self-esteem.

"Are you hurt?" Ruth called down the stairs when we could stop laughing.

"Vel, of course!" I replied with mock chagrin. "My dignity is utterly destroyed, downright gone."

We laughed some more, just two young people from oceans and worlds apart hearing angel wings gently brushing by us.

"I see the Danes and the Norwegians have met," Alf called down the stairs.

"Vel, of course," laughed Oscar.

He brushed the snow off my hair and helped me off with my coat and snow boots. Again I heard those three wonderful, first class words: "Vel, of course." I had first heard them as a red-haired, freckle-faced, battle-scarred stray kitten found by the roadside and brought home. I remembered my tongue-tied lisp as I told Pastor Nielson that my name was "Roth." But much more distinctly from the treasure house of my long-ago memories I heard the melodic sound of Mrs. Nielson's broad Danish accent, with no hesitation, saying, "Vel, of course."

But now it was a towering, dark, handsome Norseman who stood there grinning a too-large Cheshire cat grin. I wondered if I had really made a fool of myself. Was he laughing at me or with me?

"Wouldn't you know she would fall for me first thing? We Viking Norsemen always were able to conquer the Danes," Oscar jested.

"Vel, of course," I threw back at him, "but don't forget you Norwegians had to come to Denmark when you needed a really great king."

When Norway became an independent nation, the Danish king's brother gave up his Danish citizenship to become Norway's sovereign. My great-granduncle had pronounced the prayer of blessing for him as he left Denmark. The priceless oil mural of that memorable occasion still hangs in the Helsingør Museum which is visited each year by thousands of tourists.

Ruth busied herself with the dinner while I played with the baby. Oscar and Alf talked about seminary. I felt an inner contentment, a deep nearness to God, a peace that told me that God had more at stake than I did. Finally it made sense. If we seek first God's kingdom, in his own peculiar, miraculous way he will add the other "things" we need.

I was a spectator at God's miracle. Here I finally was a grown woman all dressed up like a real princess in my first honest-to-goodness store-bought ball gown complete with the red glass slippers. And here was the handsome prince of my childhood looking exactly like Rev. Koch—deep-set laughing eyes, indigo blue as the windswept fjords of his fatherland, midnight black, wavy hair, an immaculate white shirt setting off a slender blue striped tie. Oscar's pencil-slim, six-foot frame and broad shoulders were such a perfect match of Rev. Koch that I wondered in the holy of holies of my heart, *Is God playing tricks on me?*

I let my mind wander and was once more inside the elegant West Denmark church with the intricately hand-carved apostles. Briefly there flashed before me this man who had meant so much to me, only now he was not Rev. Koch whom I had mixed up with God as a child. For a moment in my mind's eye this immigrant Viking I had just met was wearing a long black robe and a handsome honeycomb collar. He was smiling down at me from the elaborately carved pulpit high on the wall of the church of my childhood as if I were indeed finally first class.

"One Norwegian *krone* for your thoughts," Oscar jested.

"You remind me of a Dane I once knew."

"A nice and very proper Dane?" he asked with a grin.

"A mighty swell first class Dane," I replied with sincerity, "one who changed my whole life."

"We Vikings are masters at doing that. We raid! We plunder! We capture beautiful blonde Danish lassies. Then we take them to our mountain caves where Thor and Odin turn them into trolls or fairy princesses."

I smiled as I remembered the Viking tales we had learned in Danish summer school.

Supper was ready. Alf's wife, Ruth, was also Danish. She was a magnetic Christian whose God-given gifts included making a humble meal on a winter evening something magical. Their immaculate student apartment was one simple room that served as kitchen, bedroom, study, living room, and nursery. There was a community bathroom down the hall. But it was easy to forget the meagerness of Ruth's domain. Her grace and charm were reflected everywhere.

Tonight the study table was adorned with sparkling snow-white linen tablecloth and napkins, elegant wedding china, glistening silverware and a single long-stemmed scarlet rose in a shimmering silver bud vase. Two tall ivory tapers flickered in silver candle holders. Ruth had placed other tapers around the room and their warmth and glow made me forget the poverty of the apartment and the winter cold outside.

The aroma of Norwegian meatballs and savory brown gravy, spicy red cabbage and steaming hot coffee brought nostalgic tears to my eyes as I remembered other winter nights in a faraway parsonage long ago.

Ruth was a nurse. She had attended nursing school with my very precious, gifted sister, who had finished Northwestern Bible School and nursing school in preparation for her call to the mission field. Oscar had met my sister briefly following Ruth and Alf's wedding. Now Oscar, whose own call was clearly etched in granite, looked quizzically at me as Ruth mentioned that my sister, who was engaged, had given up her call to the mission field. *Does he think I might do the same?* I wondered.

The evening's banter was light and pleasant and the food delectable. We cleaned up the last mouth-watering bite and finished the meal with steaming black Scandinavian coffee. Then I hugged Ruth, thanked her for the evening, and said good-bye. The baby was crying and needed to be put to sleep. I wanted to go and leave everything in the hands of One who never bungles things. If this were of God, then he would have to show me. I was not going to manipulate his will.

A friend had stopped by to pick up a paper I had typed for her, so I walked back to the dormitory with her. Back in my room I got down on my knees, but I couldn't pray. For what could I pray? After all, I already had bungled God's will once. I would have to be satisfied with the knowledge that God knew my heart *and* he knew what was best. He would make the right decision.

Outside the snow was blanketing the city. The night was still and quiet except for the tower clock on the church chiming nine.

Then the phone at the front desk rang and the house mother called my name. When I answered, I heard a warm melodic Norwegian accent on the line. It was Oscar. He said the snow was too much like Norway to waste it walking alone. Would I join him?

My reply to his invitation came easily: "Vel, of course."

It took me only seconds to don a bulky, bright red woolen sweater, throw on a jaunty red scarf and slide into my snow boots and jacket. A song in my heart, I bounded down the three flights of stairs. He was waiting at the foot of the stairs but this time I wasn't going to fall at his feet.

It was semester break and the dormitory was almost empty. I knew Alf had reserved a room for Oscar in the men's dorm next door. Some of the few remaining students had earlier laid a fire on the hearth. The immense log crackled merrily and the dorm smelled invitingly of buttery popcorn. Mother R. was examining Oscar with an approving gleam in her eye.

"It's semester break so there are no dorm hours," she told us with a knowing wink.

With Oscar beside me, the crisp winter night in Loring Park seemed magical. Snowflakes danced gracefully past the street lights. The children whose laughter had filled the park earlier that day were home tucked in their snug beds. Their snowmen stood sedately with carrot noses, coal black eyes, and worn castaway hats.

From somewhere across the ice we heard the faint sound of a radio playing the "Skaters' Waltz." Precisely matched couples were silhouetted as they skillfully waltzed on shimmering silver skates which sparkled in the lamplight. It was a group of McPhail Conservatory music students practicing for a winter ice musical. Twirl, dip, circle, pirouette, skate around the pond and back again, meet your partner, twirl, dip, circle . . .

The snow crunched under our feet. Oscar tucked my arm in his. A brilliant full moon illuminated the skaters and the towering snow-covered cedars. We walked in silence as if the night were too magical to break the spell with words.

Only the distant music and an occasional bit of laughter from the skaters interrupted the tranquil night. A night owl keeping watch from the safety of a tall pine hooted softly. I remembered the sparrow that had visited my windowsill and felt secure in knowing God always has his eye on us.

"I wonder if heaven is like this," mused Oscar. "Beautiful, peaceful, exquisitely perfect. The Vikings who sailed the seas dreamed of coming home to Valhalla, a Norwegian heaven. Valhalla is just mythology, but whenever Vikings see something this totally beautiful, when life is completely in harmony with God and could be no better, when perfect love surrounds us—we still say we are in Valhalla, kind of a heaven on earth. This is the perfection God intended for his children when he created the world."

I felt it, too, and was reluctant for the evening to end. It was getting cold as we walked back to the dormitory. The parlor fire had burned down to red embers and the few students who had been tending it had gone to bed. The quiet was broken only by the clock striking ten.

Chapter Eighteen

Something Special for Someone Special

We said our goodnights. I learned Oscar would return to Northern Baptist seminary in Chicago the next day. But he didn't seem to want to leave. The dying fire cast a warm glow on the dormitory parlor. Was he remembering a cozy cottage on a windswept land far across the sea where Hitler's men had dared hoist the hated Swastika?

Oscar's hand was on the knob when he turned to me with a stoic decisiveness I would remember long after this night.

"In Norway we don't ever waste a good fire."

It was a lame excuse and we both knew it, but why not? We were young with the world ahead of us. War was raging on battlefields around the globe but that night there was no one in the whole world but two Scandinavian warriors doing battle for God.

I shed my boots while he stoked the fire and placed another gigantic log on it before settling down on a well-worn sofa. Because I love candlelight I had provided candles for the Christmas vesper service in the dorm. They were only half burned and still lay with the matches by the hearth.

"And I don't waste good candles," I laughed as I lit a dozen in utter abandon.

"Tell me about Norway," I said as I sank into the other end of the flowered sofa. "Why did you come to America?" It seemed a safe question.

He talked of his homeland, the fishing village of Mosterhavn, the Christian Island. He told me about his devout praying Christian parents and his long journey to find God. I had never seen goats at play on the mountains or heather on the hills or fishing fleets bringing their bounty into the quay. But as Oscar described these things I remembered Papa telling me about Rosa and the Bergen flower markets and the fjords and the smell of the North Sea. I felt as if I had been there before.

He spoke nostalgically and with a bit of homesickness. "Norsemen have always sailed the seven seas. Wherever they roam, they always know that they have left a part of their hearts on the windy islands, towering mountains, and deep blue fjords. I don't know when I will ever get back, but I am sure heaven must be just like Norway. Maybe only then will I truly be home."

Then his eyes darkened as he described how the Nazis marched in and claimed his homeland. His family joined the underground resistance. His brother was shot by the Nazis. He survived and hid from them for six days without any food. Many of his countrymen were tortured in unspeakable ways. Food became so scarce that little children were eating bread made from sawdust. Earnestly and with compassion Oscar shared his gratitude for our American men who were dying on foreign soil to free his homeland.

For a while we sat in silence, our hearts bonded in a common pain. We were strangers who had just met, yet it seemed we had always known each other. I sensed Oscar was not the kind of person who would share his deepest inner sanctuary with a mere stranger. Yet he was doing just that.

"Mother prayed for me every day," he continued. "To the day she died she knew the Hound of Heaven would some day pursue me to salvation. My greatest regret is that she never saw me accept Christ.

"As she lay dying and could scarcely speak she whispered, 'I do not worry about you, Oscar. No Grindheim is ever lost. One day you will find God and when you do I know for certain God has a special dream for you to share with this cliff-hanging world.'"

There was no question that Europe was a cliff-hanging world. Martin Luther had nailed his theses on the church door and started a Reformation. Zwingli, Hubmaier, Knox, and Wesley changed the face of Europe. But succeeding generations had forgotten at what great cost their religious freedom had been won.

Ironically the great churches stood abandoned and impotent just when they were most needed. Hitler, Mussolini and Stalin were using cruel force to drive God from the continent. Europe's great composers, artists, and Reformation giants were forgotten. "I was cold and hungry, lost and needy—and you closed the church," Oscar said prophetically.

Grief-stricken by his mother's death, disturbed by a Europe that was crumbling, Oscar accepted his uncle's offer of fare to America in exchange for work on his Minnesota farm. There, far from his Christian island home, he began a pilgrimage eerily similar to mine.

"I had to find out," he explained almost inaudibly, "Who is God? Is he in charge of our lives? For what purpose did he create us? How could I know that my mother and father were really in heaven? Most of all, how could I find the dream my mother had shared with me as she was winging her way upward?"

Oscar took me back in time to a spring Minnesota morning. The meadowlarks sang in the woodbines as he drove a four-span team of sleek brown thoroughbred dray horses behind a six-row cultivator. In the distance Oscar saw his Uncle Lars running across the newly turned sod waving a piece of paper. As Lars drew closer Oscar saw it was a telegram.

Oscar's sister-in-law had died in childbirth. Tora, his brother John's wife, had been more than a sister to Oscar. She often had prayed for his soul. She had waited 12 long years for God to give her a child and now the telegram said she and the baby lay cold and dead in a common grave in the old Moster *kirkegård* (cemetery).

John was Oscar's favorite brother and his best friend. Oscar decided to return to Norway to comfort his grief-stricken brother. But what comfort could he be, he who had never found God?

Right then and there Oscar made a promise to God: "If you will take me back to Norway, I will seek you until I find you. When I do, I promise I will answer your call and serve you the rest of my days anywhere, any place you send me."

A promise keeper, just like Papa, I thought to myself.

Oscar continued, "I took the next boat and came to Haugesaund on a Sunday night just as a church full of warm and loving Christians were singing *'Du Store Gud'* ('How Great Thou Art'). I stopped to listen."

When the invitation was given, just as Papa and I had done in that old one-room church in Milltown, Oscar confessed that he was a sinner, lost and undone. He believed in Christ and Christ alone for salvation and found unspeakable joy.

"And the dream," I hardly dared ask. "You found the dream?"

The clock on the mantel chimed eleven. The embers again were burning low. I was a stranger and had no right to ask such a personal question. He would leave the next day and I might never see him again. But I longed to know. I had to know. I knew God's dream for my life; through tears and laughter I was ready to walk through dark midnights or brilliant summer mornings asking nothing but the opportunity to answer his call. Did God call others the same way along their pilgrimage to him?

Oscar did not say anything.

"I'm sorry I asked," I apologized.

He rose from the sofa to stoke the fire. "Yes, I found the dream," Oscar said quietly. He threw another log on the hearth and joined me again on the couch. Outside the winter winds were whipping the maples against the frosted window pane. It was the only sound save the crackling fire. I felt safely sheltered, as on the night Helga died and Papa stood there waiting for me to come home drenched in the cold rain of a world that was falling apart.

Outside the world still turned on its axis. Somewhere war was raging on a battlefront. But tonight the two of us were all alone in our world, alone with God, seeking his will.

Oscar shared a crystal-clear dream with me that night as the embers faded slowly on the hearth. It was a sterling dream and one that would cost me my life and my career as a college professor. It would bring the sting of being misunderstood by those for whom my call made no sense. But it would also bring a thousand times more blessings and joys and happiness than I could ever have imagined.

Slowly and reverently Oscar spoke of the church I had fallen in love with so long ago.

"In every generation, Rose, when the church was strong, when it preached Jesus and believed God's eternal Word and purposes, when it won the lost, Europe was strong and the world was safe for a while. During the Age of Enlightenment churches were filled with those who found Jesus. The immortal music of Haydn, Handel, and Bach sang God's love. Nothing could conquer Europe. She was invincible.

"Then the church began to doubt God's Word. They lost their purpose. No longer did anyone think winning the lost was the church's reason for existence. What has happened to Europe is very clearly the fault of the church. No other organization is responsible for the souls of men. No other organization is the keeper of the morals and values of a nation. If we could bring back the purpose-driven church of Jesus Christ, we could bring back Europe. It may take this war—the terrible massacre, the pain, the devastation, the concentration camps, the fear—to make it happen.

"That is my dream, and for this I will give my life. But dreams alone have never changed the world. What it will take is people like you and me who are willing without hesitation to invest every day of our lives and our very souls to prove that it can happen anywhere! When we take action, our ideas have consequences."

He hesitated, then spoke slowly and deliberately. "Jesus said we are to be the light of the world, like those candles making this room a warm and cozy bit of heaven, or the log warming our hearts on a snowy winter night. The church is to be a shelter against the cold winds of war, unbelief, hatred, torture, and concentration camps.

"I see the church as a place of unfeigned warmth and love that points men and women to Jesus. That is what the early church in Europe was. Only the church is responsible for the eternal destiny of every soul on earth. The light did not go out because Hitler marched across our land. That was merely an aftereffect. The church left and the vacuum was there for Hitler to fill.

"Because the light has gone out in the churches there is now a cold lethal darkness covering my land. When the church died, the restrictions and taboos that make civilization possible were destroyed. Hitler was free to step onto the empty stage of Europe promising to remake the world. 'Jews are our misfortunes,' Hitler said. 'When you make an omelette, you have to break some eggs.' On that pretext, millions of Jews are processed like lumps of coal headed for the furnace.

"But it is not only the Jews who have died. Europe is bombed and in shambles. Those very churches that rejected God are now burned and looted. Priests are murdered. Families are separated and children are packed off to state-run nurseries where they are taught to inform on their parents. And we did not send missionaries to Japan, so now they are sending bombs to us. Even America sits in blackouts and blinding fear. We pay no small price for letting our churches die.

"America is still first in medicine and technology and education and faith, in family and morals and values, in winning the lost world. Immigrants crowded your shores because this land was great and it was great because it was godly. Wesley sent 700 missionaries with only one instruction: 'Offer them Christ.' Hundreds of other denominations sent priests and missionaries.

"The early church leaders in America, both Roman Catholic and Protestant, built a church every covered wagon day's journey across this wonderful land. The steeples pointed predictable fingers to God. America has become the strongest and greatest nation in the world because she is founded on God. Her churches are citadels for salvation. They are winning the lost and believing God's Word! But America must take care. If America turns her back on God, doubts his Word, and neglects to win the lost, America will become a greater mission field than the darkest jungle."

The church in America could die? I thought. I remembered the night in Askov when I had been so afraid. The great organ had played and the pastor had come to my cot to pray for me. I remembered Papa and me searching for God as the church put its loving wooden arms around us. I had fallen in love with the church even before I knew God. I could not live without the church. No one could! No child in America should miss out on the church.

At every single crossroad in my life the church had been there. Let it die? Unthinkable. No other institution on earth is the keeper of eternity, of life and death. It had been a port in every storm. It seemed incredible that anyone would let that precious treasure die.

"As the saying goes, he who does not learn from history is bound to repeat it," Oscar continued urgently. He was telling me his story as if we were old friends. "We all saw what was happening. I took my last cent and bought a ticket to America. For a month I met every boat which left the harbor but Jews and refugees clamored for places and there were none.

"Hitler marched into Poland. Denmark and Norway were to be next. The boat was about to leave. The ship's list was made and the anchor was about to be hoisted when an old sea captain took me by the arm and told the authorities there was room for one more good Norseman in America. So God mercifully and miraculously put me on the very last boat to leave Norway before Hitler crushed his heavy iron heel deep on Scandinavian soil.

"The boat was crowded beyond capacity with anxious Jews and refugees fleeing for their lives. I do not take lightly that God let me escape when hundreds are being slaughtered. He would not have let me be spared unless he had some work for me to do. I have sworn that I will never rest until I find it and do it."

Oscar was not an American citizen yet (he soon would become one). It was amazing that he had seen a dream for America that I had never seen. I had never thought that Americans would be so insane as to let their churches die. I could not dream that America could become a devastated mission field. Yet I knew there was a major "God is Dead" movement sweeping the land. Seminaries were questioning the Bible and calling it a myth, devising their own rules for morals and values. Liberalism was flourishing. Church attendance was declining.

I had told God I would be willing to go to the deepest jungle in Africa, that I was willing to follow him wherever he led. But it had never entered my mind that our great first class America could become a desperate mission field, a fourth class nation.

The dormitory was silent. Outside a dog barked and an ambulance sounded muffled siren calls across the awakening metropolis. The tower clock chimed three. The candles were sputtering and the huge log was now a glowing bed of coals. We sat in silence for a long time.

I needed time to think before I answered the question I felt certain Oscar would ask about my call.

Was he wondering if I were certain that I would never abandon my call? I had seen it happen to so many. They had gone to the altar in a moment of high emotion when a missionary stirred their hearts and when going to the altar was an easy thing—even the "in thing"—to do. They had kept that call when the other missionary candidates at school made it popular—and even dramatic—to go to the mission field.

It did seem so romantic: a mission field, the jungle, being another Livingstone. But in the mundane tomorrows when the emotion had turned to reality and the price seemed too exacting, these people had turned their backs on their call. Too often, I observed these people became unhappy malcontents who always seemed to settle for fourth class.

I sat in the firelight watching the shadows play across Oscar's face. Being at Northwestern for four years, I had met many men who became good friends. We had found a platonic camaraderie which had made the days pleasant. It had been lighthearted fun, going out to a mission, singing and playing the piano, studying for exams together, splitting a nickel's worth of day-old rolls at the Crescent Bakery.

But this was something entirely different. Now in one evening, here was someone who touched my life so deeply that I knew I would never be the same. Had God really planted a holy hunch in my heart the day I first saw Oscar's picture? Maybe it was a dream, a silly, lonely young girl's romantic soap opera. I had to be sure. Too much hung in the balance to let our futures depend on imagination and feelings.

I had grown beyond a romantic schoolgirl willing to play games. If I allowed Oscar into my very soul I sensed that I would never again be able to close the door. The only one who had ever been allowed all the way into that inner sanctum of my heart and thoughts was . . . Papa.

Only Papa was with me the night the Milltown folks had sung, "I Surrender All." In the sweetness of our new-found faith I had answered a loud and resounding "Yes" to God's call on my life.

"And your call?" Oscar asked. His voice was barely audible.

I had seen him as strong and masculine, a genuine Viking warrior. But now his voice was quiet and tender and soft like a mother rocking a baby.

I hesitated to answer. The moment was too sacred, too hung between time and eternity. I sensed a presence of God's Holy Spirit so real it would guide me across life and death and years of missionary service, building churches, winning souls and bringing children into the world who would serve God.

Oscar reached his hands across the old flowered couch and took both my hands in his. But he was not merely reaching across the worn sofa but across the great wide ocean of my loneliness— across all the miles I had traveled to find God, across all the years of poverty and fleeing from trouble, across all the years when Papa and I had been outsiders, across all the memorable moments when a stronger, wiser someone had stood at the crossroads of my life assuring me that "God has something special for those who save something special for someone special." It was warm and assuring in the semidarkness, like finally coming home after a long, long journey.

I had only met this man that night, yet I was unafraid. It seemed I had met him in the yesterdays when a pastor prayed while the organ played and I fell in love with the church. I had met him in the quiet of the West Denmark Church where Rev. Koch wore his long black robe. He had been there when I had fled from sexual abuse and God had opened up another job for me. He had been

there when I had shared Christ with poor Mr.
O'Mallory. I had met him walking those five miles
to high school in the bitter, biting Minnesota winters. I had met him each time I was tempted to
drop out of high school but could not give up because I knew I had to be a promise keeper. He had
been with me the night I graduated and needed
family. He had been with me at the poor house. I
had met him when Papa had told me he was leaving for a faraway tundra. And he had been there
when God had decided John was not right and that
since I had saved something special for someone
special, out there God would have someone special for me. Yes, he had been there somewhere in
all my yesterdays. Was that why I had confused
Rev. Koch with God?

The firelight was flickering softly on his face
making him look strangely familiar, like an old
friend who was suddenly young and strong and beginning again with a dream and the courage to
turn the world back to God.

My heart overflowed with gratitude to God as
in the warm communication of silence Oscar gave
me time to walk through the many long miles of
my past, remembering all the kind and good people
who had stood at the crossroads for me, and all
the roads taken and not taken.

In the dim light the old familiar dormitory parlor look strangely like a cathedral or a beloved familiar one-room country church. Papa was kneeling beside me. He was young and full of hope and
courage to begin again because our search for God
had just ended. Now in the warmth of our close-

ness it seemed in my imagination this man I had just met was Pastor Nielson. I could see him stopping along the Jericho road binding the festering wounds of a hurting world, pouring on the healing oil with nothing more than a simple, "Vel, of course."

But then again, as the firelight played its magic I thought, *Why, he is Papa, the promise keeper, with his wonderful Scandinavian brogue.* Papa, so often misunderstood, so often fleeing from conflict yet turning around to bless those who misunderstood him. Papa—simple, wise, straightforward, honest and caring, a predictably Christian saint in work clothes. Papa, who never complained! Papa, who always spread love where there was hatred, joy where there was sadness.

My heart was overwhelmed with gratitude to Almighty God. I choked up and could not speak. Then I felt Oscar's strong arm around me. It was like a caress set to a symphony. I was no longer afraid to let him into my trysting place.

Through tears I took him home with me to Askov's magnificent church. He met Dr. Fenger and visited the old farm with its stumps and stones, the blueberries and the meadowlarks singing, and Mama coping with poverty and utter loneliness for first class. I told him of my wonderful oldest sister who cleaned a neighbor's house so we could have piano lessons.

I shared my love affair with the church, with winning the lost and with all those who had so happily brightened my way. I told him of the debt I owed, of all the wonderful lessons God had already taught me and the miracles he had wrought to bring me to this sacred hour. In the security of Oscar's arm around me it became clear to me for the very first time that ALL things—not 99 percent—work together for good to those who love the Lord (see Romans 8:28).

Every single step of my life had been preparation for tonight when my call was clearer than it had ever been. I was prepared to work with hurting children and families. I could be authentic when I told them they could make it. I owed a debt of gratitude to those who had given me a home and their hearts. I must go and do likewise. It was totally unthinkable that I, who had received so much, could ever abandon my call.

I introduced Oscar to dear sweet Mrs. Koch with her love of Bach and romance. She could make a home an elegant haven with candles and a bouquet of goldenrods on the table in the midst of a drought. I walked Oscar along the dusty country road to Milltown into the simplicity of the old one-room church where Papa and I had met Jesus face to face and I had answered a resounding lifelong "Yes!" to his call. We laughed at the gratitude cow Papa had brought for the preacher who took me in so I could attend Danish summer school.

In my eagerness to share my story, I mixed up times and places. Somewhere in this collage was the fiddle playing during the depression, the terror of seeing the church burning and God's folks fighting, Helga dying not knowing Jesus—all the patchwork quilt of my life leading to this very hour and moment when time was standing still.

We shared the Lord's prayer in Scandinavian. Oscar knew all the wonderful Danish hymns of my childhood. His mother had sung them to him in Norwegian. I had never shared with anyone but Papa the beauty of the Thorvaldson altar with Jesus with the piercing eyes and the outstretched nail-pierced hands.

Finally, it was all out. I had shared everything I had held in my heart as I waited for someone special enough to be called my confidant.

Would he think I was a fool to have bared my soul to someone I had just met, or would he sense that we had always known each other? He was going back to Chicago tomorrow and I might never see him again. He was getting up. Was he leaving?

No, he stoked the fire and gently laid on another log. It was long past time for him to go home but the log indicated he had more to say. But what? Where does one go after coming home?

"Rose, there is part of my dream I have not shared with anyone else. Tonight, after waiting ten years, I know for certain it is God's will to share it with you."

The clock on the mantle ticked quietly.

"Yes?" I said softly.

"My dream was that one day I would find someone exactly like you who would understand my dream. I've searched the world, crossed the ocean three times searching for someone who has the same dream in her heart, for unless she has, we can never really be one. I need someone like you who believes in promise keeping. For only genuine, honest-to-goodness promise keepers can turn the world and the church back to God."

The morning light was chasing away the shadows of night. The milkman was coming down the street in his jingling wagon. The city was waking up, the candles were burned low.

The sweet, sweet Spirit of Jesus flooded the room and I knew for certain this was love—for me—to the end of time. The long years of loneliness were over. I had no hesitation about discerning God's will. I curled up in Oscar's arms and reached for him with my heart and soul. This had been well worth waiting for.

"Vel, of course," I said.

For the first time in my life I was certain I was all the way home. I belonged. I was totally secure and anchored in the center of God's perfect will. I was loved with a love even greater than Papa's, surpassed only by God's love. It was a love I had searched for at every crossroad of life. Papa had prepared me for this hour. Rev. Koch and Pastor Nielson had stood by the roadside pointing the way. How I thanked God for these promise keepers.

My heart was singing for joy. It was not a winter morning. It was springtime and the trilliums were blooming in the valley. The mayflowers in the woodlands were bursting with perfume. The robins were singing in the lilac trees and the meadowlark was building his nest under the eaves of the old Milltown Baptist church. The celestial cherubs in their white robes were not on the altar of some childhood church. They were singing all around us ... singing and rejoicing ... and the great organ was playing the "Wedding March" in Valhalla.

Chapter Nineteen

Final Gifts

*T*he night was far spent and Oscar barely had time to catch the early train back to Chicago. Shakespeare said, "Love sought is good, but given unsought is better." I knew the famous bard was right. God's plan for my life had come into clear focus since this morning when God had sent his assuring wee sparrow to my window sill. All that I had waited for, saved myself for, trusted God for, the Holy spirit had made crystal clear in the deepest recesses of my heart and soul.

Outside my window in the dawn's early light the tiny sparrow once again fluttered near the warmth of my windowpane. Yes, God had his eye on me. For the first time in my life I was finally and totally home. I was no longer an outsider. I knew where I belonged.

During the months between this day and our wedding we would get to know each other better. But never once in the many long years of serving God together would either of us doubt that on this alabaster night we had received the crowning grace of humanity, the golden link which binds two hearts of love to each other and thus more closely to God. Yes, love had come unsought and brought a partner to share my life and my call.

I did not take this gift lightly. I sensed that one hour of downright love is worth a lifetime of emptiness. I would learn that love is the only service that power cannot command and money cannot buy. I would also learn that even though our marriage had been a gift from heaven God holds us responsible for the maintenance work.

Papa! I had to write Papa. With overwhelming joy I began thanking him for every mountain he had helped me climb and every valley he had led me through.

Papa would understand about the ram in the thicket. He had taught me that the promise keeper's secret is unconditional love. He had pointed the way so that now I had not missed it for myself. Papa did not seem far away but right here with me. His arms were as close as they were the day we knelt at the altar so long ago.

Papa wrote back, "Only the souls that do not love go empty in this world. Love isn't like a reservoir. You never drain it dry. It's much more like a natural spring. The longer and farther it flows, the stronger and deeper and clearer it becomes." I knew that this is what Papa worked and dreamed for Mama and all his family. It had not always been easy for him but he had never quit; he had always kept his promises. Now I knew that he rejoiced I had found this truth.

We were married in August with the beloved Dr. Moyer, President of Northwestern, performing his last marriage ceremony before God took him to glory. I shall always remember his hand on our heads as he pronounced the benediction: "The ever-living Christ is here to bless you. The nearer you keep him, the nearer you will be to one another." How I sensed Papa's presence at our wedding. It seemed that through the miles and years he was as close as he had ever been.

The next year Oscar and I spent at Northern Baptist Seminary. Then it was out to a student pastorate on the dust bowl border between Kansas and Nebraska to finish college before the final seminary degree. During those years, Oscar always added a postscript in Norwegian to my letters to Papa so that when he finally did meet Papa, no son and father could have had a closer bond than those two.

Papa's letters became less frequent and his handwriting less sure. He had spent a month in the hospital—something about his stomach. We mailed the biggest package we had ever sent. It contained heavy insulated underwear, hot chocolate mix, photos of our new church, and a long letter of hope and love. We also sent a homemade card with a long-eared beagle dog saying, "I'm lonesome without you." In my letter I begged him to come home. "Please! Papa! Please!"

They mustered him out at Bremerton Naval yards with enough of a superficial physical diagnosis of food poisoning to abandon any further responsibility for his treatment. He wrote that he would be home with Mama for Christmas. I was overjoyed. I did not have money to go home but I knew that would not be necessary. He would have family and time to get acquainted with his younger children.

I was shocked when I received a card from Papa in January written from Stockton, California, saying he was working in construction there. He was not well. I sensed something was terribly wrong and fired off a special delivery letter: "I need you Papa. Please come to us as soon as you can!"

He came posthaste. I felt like the parent-child roles were reversed. He was me in the falling snow on a wide-eyed Christmas Eve, and I was Papa bringing in the new skis. I didn't dare ask if he had missed Christmas. If he had, I felt this might be his last. If he hadn't, we had missed too many together not to have one now.

My husband cut a ceiling-high fragrant Norwegian pine and we borrowed all the church's decorations—baubles and bangles and ropes of holly and wreaths. They even had the same little shiny candle holders with candles which I remembered from my childhood. Funny how I noticed they were tin, not brass. Growing up changes things.

The little country church my husband and I were serving had given us a pounding for Christmas—a pound of this, a pound of that laid on the altar Christmas Sunday. Our student pastor's salary barely stretched from tuition to tuition, so I felt like the queen of Denmark with all that butter, sugar, eggs, coffee, and roasts. This rare opulence made it easy to cook an authentic Danish *Juleaften* Christmas Eve supper for Papa. I baked all the wonderful Danish goodies—cakes and tarts and breads.

The church caught the excitement of Papa's visit country style. When he arrived on the bus the entire congregation showed up belting out Christmas carols to the amazement of the bus driver and a much older Papa who stepped into my life as if he had not been away for an eternity.

I kept him waiting on our front porch until my husband lit all the candles. Yes, Papa was now the childlike recipient of the mystical birth on a Judean plain long ago and I was Papa with the skis wanting so much to make it all real.

The tree was stacked high with sweaters, socks, books, and mittens brought by the congregation. Being a country pastor is a treat nobody should miss!

The denomination's executives had consoled my husband when they sent him to an all-but-empty church by saying they could probably pay his salary for the two years he had left in college. Just preach and keep it open was all they asked. But in all his years of ministry my husband never saw an empty church, just lots of lost people needing Christ. When he saw the after-school herd that came thundering down the hill right past the church door he announced the opening of a kids' club.

By the time of Papa's visit, two years and lots
of hard work later, after several hundred children,
youth, and families had accepted Christ, the
church was packed. Building a youth center was
essential and Papa, who would never take charity, offered to stay to help with the construction.
How thrilled I was for anything that would keep
him with us longer.

That January was snowbound and nobody
could work. I was so glad! While my husband was
away at college, I piled corn cobs and kindling in
the old kitchen cook stove, pulled up two ancient
rockers, shut the door on the rest of the cold house
and Papa and I were back in Askov.

What a joy to walk through sixty-five years of
Papa's pilgrimage. It was the benediction to a
much too long separation. We were two adults
walking down the same road together all the way
from Denmark to the Aleutian Islands. Only this
time I was protecting Papa, keeping him warm
and fed and loved. I wanted to shelter him from
all the storms he had ever weathered.

We both had a sense of finality as if what we
had to say we needed to say quickly—now. He
showed me savings bonds which would mature at
$40,000 just in time to make sure the four younger
children did not have to struggle to get an education. (Unfortunately, when that time came Papa
was gone and so was the money, so none of them
got to graduate from a four-year college. I regretted that. My two younger sisters, though enormously gifted, spent their lives serving God well
but working for minimal wages. My precious

younger brother did go to Bible school and became an outstanding missionary pilot. My service to God could never begin to equal his. My youngest brother's body was never recovered from Lake Chelan where he drowned when he was sixteen, before he could even finish high school.)

I cooked all Papa's favorites but apologetically he just wanted warm milk and toast, and he had trouble with that. The days passed too swiftly. I savored every one, holding them close to my heart against a day I pushed out of my thinking.

On what turned out to be the last day of his visit, even though Papa had been unwilling to talk about being old or sick, I knew I had to ask, "Papa, what's wrong?"

We sat in that snowbound, creaking parsonage for an eternity, an old, spent warrior and his loving protégé. We listened to the wind bellow and moan for a long time. I was about to get up to feed corn cobs to the old cook stove when Papa slowly and deliberately took my hand in his.

"There's a lump in my stomach."

I felt it and it was big and hard. Nothing had ever come between us before, but now I felt a too-impatient enemy neither Papa nor I knew how to defy was knocking at the door. Drought and grasshoppers, winter storms and depression we had been able to conquer—but this was something much more obstinate. Against this we had only our faith, love, and prayers. Would they be enough?

Like on the night of my high school graduation, I wanted to keep him close to me, but I knew he had to go to the Mayo Clinic at once. My husband

and I took him to the train station. I hugged him close. The conductor called "All aboard" as Papa pressed a weather-beaten envelope into my hand.

We waved to him through the morning fog, standing alone on the empty railroad platform until the winter whiteness and the flood of tears blinded us to the last vestige of the train which had taken Papa from us.

Reluctantly, we walked silently arm in arm up Main Street, back to the strangely empty parsonage to open the letter. It was my high school diploma! Papa had kept it in his wallet all those years. Did he know he would not need it any more?

Papa had one more gift for me. He had left behind the little steamer trunk which had followed him through all the years. It contained Mama and Papa's wedding picture and all the letters I had written to him over the years. In his feeble handwriting he had penned me his final note:

Dearest Rose, "We have seen too many stars to fear the night." *Jeg elsker dig i evihedet,* (I will love you through eternity). Papa

Chapter Twenty

Going Home

The hospital sent Papa home to die. Before I went home to see him for the last time, my husband graciously helped me overcome a barrier that could have hindered our ministry for life.

Oscar said, "Rose, you have always felt you were treated as a fourth class outsider because you loved Papa. Unforgiveness is like a load of manure you carry around with you. It not only complicates your life, it touches everyone around you. Go and make peace with your mother before Papa dies."

It was a wise decision and I was glad Papa saw me do it. The years ahead gave Mama both a Gethsemane and an Easter. After my youngest brother was tragically drowned Mama had a new spiritual awakening. She who was manor born spent her last days as a Mother Teresa nursing the least and the last and the lonely at the Union Gospel Mission. I'm sure up in heaven Papa looked down with joy to see that Mama had also become a promise keeper.

She lived to past ninety and during her last years I flew to visit her often. We read the old Danish Bible and sang the songs of her childhood. I learned to better understand Mama's journey through stumps and stones, depression, tornadoes, and death. Yes, Oscar had been right and I was glad I had been able to give both Papa and Mama this as my final gift to them both. Truly, God gives us the gift of memory so we can enjoy roses in December.

Papa failed fast. He picked out a plot under a majestic oak. As his time became shorter, he asked me to play the songs he wanted at his funeral: "Blessed Assurance, Jesus Is Mine!" and the old Danish hymn, *Du Store Gud* (How Great Thou Art). We shared Psalms from his Danish Bible. There was nothing more to say. There was nothing left to do. It had all been said and done, and I was glad. That's the way two very best friends need to part.

I will always carry in my heart the glow of that death.

Papa had been in great pain and was unable to speak until sunset of the day he died. The sunlight from the last brilliant burst of the day streamed into his room with a blaze of exuberance. Outside enormous cumulous clouds painted the sky. Papa gallantly lifted his cancer-ridden body from the pillow. Elevating a bony finger to Jesus, a smile brighter than the evening sun illuminated his dying face.

With a clarion, unfaltering voice—the voice of the Papa I had known so long ago—Papa used his very last words to witness to the One who had given him life and peace.

"I have just had a vision or a dream," he began. "I saw Jesus in those clouds right up there. His face was full of joy and glory. His hands with the nail prints were stretched out to me. And he said, 'Holger, come home. Your sins are all forgiven.' "

In my mind's eye, I saw Thorvaldson's Jesus which had decorated the church altars of my childhood.

Papa never spoke again. He lay back on the pillows and was finally at home with Jesus . . . and Rosa . . . and hopefully Helga. Without a single doubt, now Papa was finally and indisputably first class.

If I have ever been tempted to forget my call, all I have to do is to remember that everyone I meet must die the way Papa died—first class with assurance in their hearts that Jesus makes them first class, fit for heaven. Christ is the answer and I just have to tell them. I sorely missed Papa but I knew the lessons he had taught me would be with me always, that I would hand them down to my children and hopefully they would to theirs.

A poem by the Danish poet B.S. Ingeman was written at the foot of the Askov altar. It read:

Såret jeg flyet fra Ulvens Tand,
Mit Blod til hand Fod er rundet
Selv Han bar mig til Kildens Rand,
Der had jeg Lægedom fundet.

Wounded and left by the wolf to die,
He found me and tenderly gave me
Comfort and care at the fountain, where I
Live by his love who has saved me.

That was Papa's eulogy.

Postscript

$\mathcal{F}$ or twenty-seven years, until his untimely death from Lou Gehrig's disease, Oscar's mission field was the dying churches of America. He won the Baptists' highest national award as an outstanding minister in America for reviving dying and declining churches.

His last words to me were, "Make America see it can happen anywhere!"

Reluctantly, though I had five children and was teaching at a college, I picked up his mantle and continued his work. In 1987 the United Methodist Church gave me their highest national award, the Circuit Rider Award, as outstanding United Methodist missionary in America for reviving churches. I now speak and write around the world and am seeing miracles happen in church after church. The autobiography of our life together is told in the award-winning book, *New Life for Dying Churches! It Can Happen Anywhere,* which won the international award as best nonfiction and was filmed by Ken Anderson Films. Along with James Kennedy's video "Say it with Confidence," workbooks, and texts it is the basis for an eight-hour do-it-yourself Church Growth Seminar which is doubling churches' memberships worldwide.

My new husband, Jim Sims, and I reside at 34631 Orchid Parkway, Ridge Manor, Florida 33525 (904/583-3358).

Photo Album

Left: *Papa, my best friend!* Right: *Rose is age nine in this photo. It was the middle of the Great Depression and the year Helga died.*

*Holger Voetmann (age 34) and Else Fenger (age 24)
were married March 20, 1914 in Iowa.*

Rev. & Mrs. Holger Koch and family, about 1929. He was pastor of the West Denmark Lutheran Church in Luck, Wisconsin, when Rose came to stay with the parsonage family.

Rose Fenger Voetmann, 1944
This photo was taken during her first year at North-
western Bible School and Seminary in Minneapolis.
Papa was working in the Aleutian Islands.

Oscar Johan Grindheim, 1944
Oscar was 35 when this photo was taken during the
summer before he and Rose met. He spent that sum-
mer pastoring the Brooklyn, New York, Norwegian
Baptist Church.

Papa plowing the virgin soil of Askov, Minnesota, 1921.

Rev. B. Emil and Mary Nielson, 1930. He was pastor of Milltown Baptist Church in Milltown, Wisconsin. The Nielsons' "Vel, of course!" religion influences Rose's life to this day.

Mama and I became close friends before she went home to join Papa. Here we are when she was 92.